IN THE
R A B B I S'
Garden

IN THE
R A B B I S'
Garden

ADAM AND EVE IN THE MIDRASH

GERALD J. BLIDSTEIN

JASON ARONSON INC.
Northvale, New Jersey
Jerusalem

The author gratefully acknowledges permission to use the following:

The Holy Scriptures. (1917) pp. 5–6, Copyright © 1917 The Jewish Publication Society. Used by permission of the publisher.

Midrash Rabbah, vol. 1. (1983) ed. by Freedman & Simon. Copyright © 1983 by The Soncino Press, Ltd. Used by permission of the publisher.

This book was set in 12 pt. Berkeley Oldstyle Book by Alabama Book Composition of Deatsville, Alabama, and printed and bound by Book-mart Press of North Bergen, New Jersey.

Library of Congress Cataloging-in-Publication Data

Blidstein, Gerald J.
    In the rabbis' garden : Adam and Eve in the midrash / by Gerald J.
Blidstein.
        p.   cm.
    Includes bibliographical references and index.
    ISBN 0-7657-5987-X (alk. paper)
    1. Adam (Biblical figure) in rabbinical literature.   2. Eve
(Biblical figure) in rabbinical literature.   3. Bible.   O.T.
Genesis III, 1–12 — Criticism, interpretation, etc.   4. Midrash
rabbah.   Genesis XVIII–XIX — Criticism, interpretation, etc.
I. Title.
BM518.A4B55   1997
296.1'4206–dc21   97-408
                                                                CIP

Manufactured in the United States of America. Jason Aronson Inc. offers books and cassettes. For information and catalog write to Jason Aronson Inc., 230 Livingston Street, Northvale, NJ 07647.

CONTENTS

ACKNOWLEDGMENTS

The midrashic texts discussed in this book are all taken from *Bereshit Rabbah*, a compilation edited in the Land of Israel, roughly in the mid-fourth century. The material found in this *midrash* most likely derives from the late first century on. All of the material comes from the nineteenth *parasha* (except for the first, which is from the eighteenth *parasha*) and discusses the twelve verses, Genesis 3:1–12. They represent the midrashic material found in the current printed editions of the original Hebrew texts. Passages from Genesis, chapter 3, have been presented according to the translations in the Jewish Publication Society's *The Holy Scriptures* (Philadelphia, 1917), with the permission of J. P. S. Passages from *Genesis Rabbah* have been included, with minor revisions, according to H. Freedman and M. Simon, *Midrash Rabbah*, volume 1 (London: Soncino Press, 1939), pp. 147–159, with the permission of Soncino Press.

FOREWORD

In the Rabbis' Garden: The Midrash *on Adam and Eve* is a contemporary reflection on the midrashic comments to the story of Adam and Eve. It interprets—and reacts to—*midrash* that touches on the basic aspects of the human condition: guilt, virtue, responsibility, God, death, and sexuality, all rooted in the primal experience of Eden.

∾

The story of Adam and Eve has long been with us as a basic document of the human condition. It tells of the creation of life and the imposition of death, of the experience of sin and punishment, and of mutuality and betrayal, obedience and rebellion, fear and hope, culture and nature, woman and man, God and humanity. All the while, we are dealing with text, biblical words, sentences, paragraphs, with narrative, and dialogue.

The biblical text has stimulated *midrash*, a searching process that fills in gaps, exposes levels of meaning, stretches the imagination, solves problems—and creates new ones. Fragmentary as they are, the midrashic comments illumine the text and the human situation.

The persons of Adam, Eve, and the serpent are fleshed out, as are their motivations. Who are they? What wisdom does human-kind hope to gain, and what is wisdom's ultimate worth? What drives the serpent? What is God's part? What role does sexuality play in the drama of the first sin? And what role the mutuality of Adam and Eve? Where does death come in? And the lesser details: what of the fruit, and why the focus on clothing?

The midrashic readings walk the borders of psychology and philosophy, literature and religion, and speak with a voice that is knowing and contemporary, committed yet sophisticated. We assume that these readings are not historically determined or limited, but rather are part of the conversation that Jews have carried on with the Bible from ancient times and continue to carry on today. In listening to the midrashic voice, we also interpret it, since the comments are themselves fragmentary, challenging, frequently enigmatic, and often suggestive. To listen is to become engaged. And we interpret and reflect as modern, persons who are eager to hear a voice that is, uncannily, both ancient and contemporary.

INTRODUCTION

For the last two millennia, the text of the Garden of Eden and the traditions of its interpretations have provided the rarely disputed basis from which our explanations of the nature and status of humankind have been derived. Our primary relationships— between man and woman, humanity and deity, and humanity and nature—have been defined by our understanding of this biblical text. Our conceptions of perfection and our experiences of imperfection have been . . . understood . . . in terms of the Genesis story. . . . The Garden narrative has been central in informing both the meaning and the content of our sexual, moral, artistic, and literary traditions. The Eden story can be seen as the text of Western men and women. . . .

The text still haunts us. This puzzling, question-raising, and meaning-overloaded text with its mysterious trees and talking snake. . . .

So writes Paul Morris about those first chapters of Genesis, their formative impact and concrete simplicity, and their tantalizing, teasing mystery.

Certainly, the Jewish tradition—if we may mount so brazen a generalization—approaches the Genesis narrative differently than does Christianity. Morris's description more aptly fits the Christian appropriation. Adam and Eve are, quite frankly, less central to Judaism as a whole, which finds its foundational figures and locates its significant narrative elsewhere. Even regarding the event in Eden, Judaism focuses on different moments, explores different options, and asks different questions. Classical Judaism, after all, sets the idea of God's command (*mitzvah*) at the center of its religious consciousness; this will certainly influence its understanding of what God first requires of Adam and Eve. Classical Judaism is also fully committed to the legitimacy of human sexuality and marriage—and that will influence its discussion of the relationship between first man and woman, as well as its understanding of their encounter with sin and the snake. Perhaps, too, Judaism is less given to reading the narrative as the story of how humanity degenerated, and is more likely to read it as being descriptive of what the human situation is and always has been: less primal history or lost ideal, and more existential reality. Do we dream of a return to Eden?

This is not intended to minimize the universal significance of the text. Universal meanings always emerge out of specific modes of reading and experience. These midrashic readings explore the the basic conditions of the human situation, as is appropriate in a discussion of that most basic of all narratives—Adam and Eve in the Garden of Eden. The focus is on *psyche* and *mythos*—that is, on human nature and humanity's intercourse with the divine, stripped bare. Indeed, these *midrashim* are perhaps the most distilled, concentrated examples of rabbinic explorations into the basic conditions of human existence and experience. At the same time, the rabbis draw on their own experience and reflect upon it; and this experience is, of course, human and Jewish, universal and historically specific.

I use the term midrashic *readings* deliberately. *Midrash* is not
doctrinaire, even in its basic structure, typically presenting a
variety of comments on any given point, inviting the reader to
choose, or, more precisely, to browse or to taste—to move on, or
perhaps to remain and add to what he has found. (I have
probably done all of these.) *Midrash* is a discussion of, and with,
the biblical text, but it is also an internal conversation, of the
masters among themselves, across centuries.

In how many ways does *midrash* read the Bible? Too many to
tell. It can approach the text in the most outrageous manner,
foisting absolutely impossible meanings on long-suffering words
and phrases, splitting coherent units and combining patently
discrete ones. Beginning readers are often baffled, disoriented,
and disturbed. At the same time, *midrash* can produce the most
delicately accurate readings of the Bible, awakening us to see gaps
within a seemingly seamless whole and to hear echoes of distant
passages. It is a textual commentary and requires its readers to
grapple with the biblical text; at the same time, it deals in
concrete images and mystifying parables that require its readers
to extract meaning from experience. It reads very literally, but it
never renounces the imagination. It hugs the ground, even when
it soars.

The *midrashim* that I explore in this volume discuss the
narrative from the point at which the snake enters and accompany the tale until Adam and Eve confess their sins. I focus on the
motivations that called the sin into existence; on the dynamics of
snake, man, and woman, and their intentions toward each other;
on humanity before "the knowledge of good and evil" and
subsequent to it; and on the experience of God's presence—
commanding, caring, confounding—in the Garden. Sin and
regret, lust, hope, responsibility, loyalty, authority, betrayal, fear,
ambition, appetite, growth, understanding, nature and culture,
ethics and myth, the banishment of the people Israel from its

land, and even the wise exercise of rabbinic authority—these all come into play. So do the seemingly minor aspects: the fruit, the issue of clothing.

What have I done in my explorations? Where do I lead the reader? This is difficult to sum up. Sometimes I try to explain how the *midrash* treats the biblical text, and those explications do not escape technicalities. At other times, I try to plumb the content and significance of the midrashic teaching, freed of its literary complications. Generally, I ask the *midrash* questions; I probe and nudge it further than it thinks of going. So this little volume is not exactly a commentary; it is, equally, a *midrash* on a *midrash*.

Years ago I promised my children I would take a break from academic writing and do a book for them. They were, after all, too young then to understand (or find interest in) scholarship. It has taken me a long time to fulfill that promise. I have not written a story, but reflections of reflections on a story, so I have only partially kept my promise. To reflect on *midrash*, certainly on Genesis itself, is the least juvenile of activities. But the children, too, are now adults or are entering adulthood. The book was written in the spring and summer of 1994.

Beersheba, 1997

GENESIS
2:25 AND 3:1-24

And they were both naked, the man and his wife, and were not ashamed.

Now the serpent was more subtle than any beast of the field which the LORD God had made. And he said unto the woman: "Yea, hath God said: Ye shall not eat of any tree of the garden?" And the woman said unto the serpent: "Of the fruit of the trees of the garden we may eat; but of the fruit of the tree which is in the midst of the garden, God hath said: Ye shall not eat of it, neither shall ye touch it, lest ye die." And the serpent said unto the woman: "Ye shall not surely die; for God doth know that in the day ye eat thereof, then your eyes shall be opened, and ye shall be as God, knowing good and evil." And when the woman saw that the tree was good for food, and that it was a delight to the eyes and that the tree was to be desired to make one wise, she took of the fruit thereof, and did eat; and she gave unto her husband with her, and he did eat. And the eyes of them both were opened, and they knew that they were naked; and they sewed fig leaves together, and made themselves girdles. And they heard the voice of the LORD God walking in the garden toward the cool of the day; and the man and his wife hid themselves from the presence of the LORD God amongst the trees of the garden. And the Lord God called unto the man and said unto him: "Where art thou?" And he said: "I heard Thy voice in the garden, and I was afraid, because I was naked; and I hid myself." And He said: "Who told thee that thou wast naked? Hast thou eaten of the tree, whereof of I commanded thee that thou shouldst not eat?" And the man said: "The woman whom Thou gavest to be with me, she gave me of the tree, and I did eat." And the LORD God said unto the woman: "What is this thou hast done?" And the woman said: "The serpent beguiled me, and I did eat." And the LORD God said unto the serpent: "Because thou has done this, cursed art thou from among all cattle, and from among all beasts of the field; upon thy belly shalt thou go, and dust shalt thou eat all the days of thy life. And I will put enmity between thee and the woman, and between thy seed and her seed; they shall bruise thy head, and thou shalt bruise their heel."

Unto the woman He said: "I will greatly multiply thy pain and thy travail; in pain thou shalt bring forth children; and thy desire shall be to thy husband, and he shall rule over thee."

And unto Adam He said: "Because thou hast hearkened unto the voice of thy wife, and hast eaten of the tree, of which I commanded thee, saying: Thou shalt not eat of it; cursed is the ground for thy sake; in toil shalt thou eat of it all the days of thy life. Thorns also and thistles shall it bring forth to thee; and thou shalt eat the herb of the field. In the sweat of thy face shalt thou eat bread, till thou return unto the ground; for out of it wast thou taken; for dust thou art, and unto dust shalt thou return." And the man called his wife's name Eve; because she was the mother of all living. And the LORD God made for Adam and for his wife garments of skins, and clothed them.

And the LORD God said: "Behold, the man is become as one of us, to know good and evil, and now, lest he put forth his hand, and take also of the tree of life, and eat and live for ever." Therefore the LORD God sent him forth from the garden of Eden, to till the ground from whence he was taken. So He drove out the man; and He placed at the east of the garden of Eden the cherubim, and the flaming sword which turned every way, to keep the way to the tree of life. (Genesis 2:25 and 3:1–24)

LUST

"And they were not ashamed. Now the serpent was more subtle . . ." Now, surely Scripture should have stated, "And the Lord God made for Adam and his wife garments of skin" (Genesis 3:21) [immediately after the former verse]? Said R. Joshua b. Karhah: It teaches you through what sin that wicked creature inveigled them. Because he saw them engaged in intercourse, he [the serpent] conceived a passion for her. R. Jacob of Kefar Hanan said: It is thus written in order not to conclude with the passage on the serpent.

—Genesis Rabbah 18:6

According to the straightforward meaning of the biblical narrative, God makes clothes for Adam and Eve *after* they sin. Having eaten of the forbidden tree and having discovered their nakedness, the two have sewn garments of fig leaves, but these will not suffice—not for the different, rougher world they now enter. So God provides them with clothing before He exiles them from the Garden. This sequence (Genesis 3:7, 3:10–11, and 3:17–24)

1

strikes a balancing, compassionate note: having just cursed man, woman, and earth, God provides for His creatures. He will exile them from His garden, but they will leave wearing the clothes that He has provided for them and carrying the dual message of His parental anger and love.

But the midrashic question apparently assumes that God made "garments of skin" for Adam and Eve immediately after their creation, *before* they sin. This assumption mangles the narrative: how do Adam and Eve "discover their nakedness" after they sin, if they are, in fact, already clothed? (Are clothes, perhaps, essential to the perception of nakedness?) And why sew clothes from fig leaves? Textually, why assume that Genesis 3:21 describes an event that, in fact, took place earlier (only to be inserted into the biblical text later)? Most significantly, why should God provide "garments of skin," if these first humans were created (by Him!) "not ashamed"?

One frequent suggestion is that these "garments of skin" are, in fact, the "garments of light" that we shall encounter in other midrashic traditions and are not physical clothes at all. Spiritual "garments of light" are, of course, completely irrelevant to problems of physical nakedness; therefore, the above questions become similarly irrelevant. But spiritual garments would be equally irrelevant to the serpent's peeping at Adam and Eve at love. More significantly, creatures who wear "garments of light" probably have no carnal experiences at all; yet our *midrash* plants Adam and Eve firmly in the physical universe. So we are back to our earlier reading, with a midrashic questioner who assumes that God provided Adam and Eve with clothes—real clothes— immediately after their creation.

Another, less dramatic, possibility is that the questioner does not suggest a change in the sequence of events. His point is thematic. God's provision of garments of skin—after the sin— does, in fact, solve the problem of human nakedness and change the condition of First Man and Woman, as it is described at the end of Genesis 2. Why not report this development, he asks, before it actually happens but where it is contextually relevant?

The *midrash* provides two solutions to its query. R. Jacob of Kefar Hanan agrees that God's provision of garments to Adam and Eve ought to have been reported at the end of Genesis 2, before the sin and its subsequent fallout. It is not recorded then, simply because it would have been poor form—ominous, even—to end humankind's experience in the Garden of Eden with the divine curses and the serpent's success. This is how the passage would have ended without the mention of God giving clothes to humanity. It is much better to conclude instead with God's loving concern for our first ancestors. (Such benevolent form continues to inform Jewish practice, which generally avoids either beginning or ending a Torah-reading in synagogue with negative statements.) This solution is purely structural; it does not interact at all with the actual events described by the text.

R. Joshua ben Karhah's solution, on the other hand, presumes a dynamic relationship between the text and its events. By omitting mention of their clothes, the Bible intends to emphatically say that Adam and Eve were, in fact, naked. And, since we are expected to know that they were initially clothed by God, this nakedness can only mean that they had taken their clothes off and were making love. It then juxtaposes the couple's nakedness with the serpent's presence. The text has meaning, then, not only in what it says, but in what it omits; indeed, omission can sometimes even imply activity.

By eliminating mention of God's provision of clothes for Adam and Eve, R. Joshua b. Karhah claims, the Bible focuses on their nakedness. This focus provides the motive for the serpent's attraction to the human pair and his successful assault upon their virtue. This "nakedness" has, in truth, been read in different ways. It has been taken to indicate a "human relationship characterized by innocence and mutual trust" (Lambden), or as signifying "defenselessness and helplessness, without possessions or power" (J. Magonet). Certainly, all these characteristics led smoothly to the serpent's assault. For R. Joshua, though, the nakedness of Adam and Eve suggests their sexuality (if there is sexuality where there is no shame) and so, undoubtedly, does the comment that "they were not ashamed." It is this sexuality that attracts the serpent and to which he responds. The serpent, moreover, is emphatically male—a fact that, although subtly present in the Bible, is not stressed as it is here.

The sexual context of the entire episode may even be suggested by the verses preceding the temptation story as a whole: "Hence a man leaves his father and mother and clings to his wife, so that they become one flesh. The two of them were naked, the man and his wife, yet they felt no shame. Now the serpent was the shrewdest of all the wild beasts that the Lord had made" (Genesis 2:24–3:1; the Hebrew text has no chapter division at this point). The serpent is introduced immediately after the description of the pair's innocent nakedness, which itself follows on the statement that the man and his wife "become one flesh." Nor could the *midrash* have missed the fact that the letters rendered here as "subtle" can, if vocalized differently, meaning "naked." This now provides a matrix for the serpent's behavior, although the *midrash* is undoubtedly moved by its own ethical agenda no less than by the biblical context.

The sexuality of the first pair while yet in the Garden of Eden is apparent in this and many other—though not all—midrashic texts. Here, sexuality is not a sin or the product of sin; it is certainly not the Original Sin. The *midrash* [even accepting this translation of a difficult term] does state: "through what sin did that wicked creature inveigle them." But, given the drift of the passage as a whole, I would say that the "sin" referred to is not legitimate sexual union, but rather illegitimate passion and sexual jealousy. The Serpent is the intruder, the adulterous third party. The serpent's sin, therefore, is ethical—even halakhic. His attraction to Eve, moreover, is exclusively sexual, stimulated by his voyeuristic experience. His passion is purely physical. In some midrashic traditions, he lusted after both Adam and Eve.

The voyeuristic aspect of the serpent returns us to the biblical phrase "and they were not ashamed." Adam and Eve felt no shame in exposure, in being seen—by each other, or even by others. The serpent, however, does know shame, since he is aroused when he watches the couple. The reality of "observation" already exists. For R. Joshua's serpent, lust already exists.

The serpent's project is not simple. Wishing to possess Eve, he must dispose of Adam—that much is clear. Eve must stay alive, she must not suffer Adam's death, if the serpent is to realize his plan. To further complicate matters, the serpent is convinced that his way to Adam lies through Eve—a rather tortuous route. In fact, the serpent does succeed in seducing both Adam and Eve, but his success is only partial—not merely because God punished all of them, but, more to the point of the midrashic narrative, because Eve willingly shares Adam's fate. She turns against the serpent, becoming its prime accuser—perhaps the most cruel turn of events for that creature in its midrashic mode.

It is more difficult, as I have said, to reconstruct the serpent's wishful thinking. Part of the midrashic message may indeed be that lust always plays upon the imagination, upon wishful thinking (including the wishful thought that Eve would join the serpent after he caused Adam's death, with her collaboration, innocent or otherwise!). Be that as it may, one must assume that the serpent thought that Eve would not be punished, only Adam—and that she would be left alive with him.

There is a more radical reading. Perhaps we should not assume that the serpent's conversation with Eve was only a way of convincing her, and Adam through her, to eat of the fruit. The conversation itself is already part of the forbidden experience— communication, personal intercourse with the serpent, who thus gains his goal. Later midrashic traditions (as well as earlier Second Commonwealth traditions) read Eve's eating of the forbidden fruit as an act of sexual intercourse with the serpent. Perhaps this lies at the root of our *midrash*, too. If that is the case, the lusting serpent does not anticipate a continuing relationship but dreams rather of immediate satisfaction.

∾

Our *midrash*—this text and the collection in which it is found— does not raise the most troubling questions about the serpent. Why is there an evil creature in Eden before the sin, before humankind's initial disobedience? Where does Evil come from, then? Does the serpent embody an evil principle, an entity in basic conflict with the good creator of Eden and humankind? True, God will punish the serpent and curse him at day's end, but perhaps this is merely the conclusion of one day's skirmish in a continuing war. More to the point, the Bible reports that the serpent was "the shrewdest of all the wild beasts that the Lord God had made"—so we know that he was a creature created by God, not His equal.

By posing these questions—and expecting that they will be answered—we virtually invite the perspective found in pre-rabbinic Jewish material of the Second Commonwealth (as well as in early Christian texts and later rabbinic works) and the legends in which it is embodied. Here, the serpent is Satan's man; he speaks for his master. In more abstract discussion, the "primeval serpent" (as he is called in even some midrashic texts) represents a cosmic, metaphysical entity or principle. Evil, then, is not merely a humanly dysfunctional activity; it is part of the very structure of being—although it does have a special early affinity for humans.

Our *midrash*, however, prefers to treat the serpent on the ethical level: he is the creature who lusts for Eve. It is possible that lust has a metaphysical root, but that is not the midrashic concern. Its emphasis is that lust leads to evil, not that evil leads to lust. True, it is likely that this creature was no innocent, that he deliberately peeped. But even then, the focus is not on the metaphysics of universal sin but on its psychological dynamics. If so, the midrashic serpent is virtually a symbol of humanity. This reading of the serpent (or perhaps I should say: this staging of the serpent) as the *alter ego* of Adam and Eve (rather than as their opposite) enables the *midrash* to say much more than it otherwise could about human failure and corruption.

This text sees a sexual motive for the serpent's maneuver. Other texts also know of the serpent's lust for Eve, but they integrate it into a broader pattern of sin.

What was the wicked serpent contemplating at the time? He thought: I shall go and kill Adam and wed his wife, and I shall be king over the whole world. I shall walk with upright posture and eat all the world's dainties. Said the Holy One, blessed be He, to him: Your thought was, I shall kill Adam and wed Eve; therefore, "I will put enmity between you and the woman" (Genesis

> 3:15). Your thought was, I shall be king over the
> whole world; therefore, "cursed are you among all
> cattle" (Genesis 3:14). Your thought was, I shall
> walk with upright posture, therefore, "upon thy
> belly shall you go." Your thought was, I shall eat
> all the world's dainties, therefore "dust shall you
> eat all the days of your life." (*Fathers According to
> R. Nathan*, version A, chapter 1 [trans. J. Golding,
> p. 10])

The serpent's sin lies in his unruly ambition, his desire to reach
beyond his proper station and status, his rejection of the limits
set. Fundamentally, he wishes to become fully human, to usurp
Adam's role vis-à-vis the rest of the world, and to supplant Adam
in Eve's affections. Ambition, as exemplified by the midrashic
serpent, is not found in the disadvantaged. The serpent already
has much; he is king of all the other creatures ("shrewdest of all
the creatures"), and so on. That, of course, only whets his
appetite to reach for the rung above.

The serpent's sins are disclosed, literarily, in the punishments
he receives. Each punishment is appropriate to its specific sin, as
God patiently explains; "measure for measure" is already the
modality of punishment in primeval Eden. As to the character of
the sin, our *midrash* does give pride of place to illegitimate sexual
passion, but the serpent's lust really seems to embody a broader
thrust:

> . . . the primeval serpent set its eyes on that
> which was not proper for it; what it sought was
> not granted to it and what it possessed was taken
> from it. The Holy One, blessed be He, said, I
> declared, Let it be king over every animal and
> beast, but now: "Cursed are you above all cattle

and above every beast of the field." I declared,
Let it walk with an erect posture, but now it shall
go upon its belly; I declared, Let its food be the
same as that of man, but now it shall eat dust. It
said, I will kill Adam and marry Eve, but now:
"I will put enmity between between you and the
woman. . . ." Similarly, do we find with Cain,
Korah, Balaam . . . who set their eyes on what
was not proper for them—what they sought was
not granted to them and what they possessed was
taken from them. (Babylonian Talmud, *Sotah* 9b)

The serpent, here, possesses virtually human characteristics:
rule, upright posture, food. This description is not all that remote
from the implications of the biblical story. True, the serpent is
only "more subtle than all the other beasts" in the Bible, so
perhaps he only represents the upper register of the animal
world. Indeed, even if the serpent is cursed after the sin to eat
dust and crawl on his belly, we might want to infer only that he
walked and ate proper food before. But there is an ambiguity
here—perhaps he walked absolutely erect and ate prepared
food? And if he speaks as humans do and knows much about
divine motives and plans, he is likely closer to man than to beast.
He loses it all, though, because of his "improper" desire for
Eve. If this is the moral, his desire is probably not simple lust but
rather jealousy, the wish to possess that which is another's—in
this case, that which symbolizes the essential chasm between
Adam and the serpent. The serpent already possesses all that is
human, except for the relationship with Eve; and, as with Cain,
Korah, and the others, it is not what is possessed that whets the
appetite but what is not possessed. (So, too, in its talmudic
context, this teaching is applied to the case of the adulterous
wife—she loses both her husband and her paramour.) This

would describe the first human pair as well—both their sin and their punishment. Indeed, the omission of Adam and Eve from the list of biblical characters who lost what they had in their desire to gain what was not given them probably means that they are included with the serpent, whose sin is even more emphatically made a paradigm for human behavior and fate.

It is obvious that the broad idea of serpentine overreaching was generated not from the punishments inflicted upon him—which did provide the specifics—but rather from what is said about his human counterpart. Perhaps a more subtle form of this claim would be that it is generated from the substance of the serpent's successful seduction of Adam and Eve themselves. He tempts them, after all, "as soon as you eat . . . your eyes will be opened and you will be like God, who knows good and evil" (Genesis 3:5). Humankind, too, wishes to be more than man and woman; it desires to be "like God." The root of our parents' sin is this yearning, not the desire to disobey, or even to rebel. The serpent knew to tempt humanity with the same overreaching that he recognized in himself—thus, perhaps, the construction of the midrashic narrative.

There may well be a difference between the yearning to be "as God" and the desire to wed Eve. The former is noble; the latter, tawdry. Indeed, it almost seems trivial. It is saved from triviality by the midrashic reminder that the serpent also connived to murder Adam. But the next human sin, Cain's, *is*, in fact, murder and it, too, is fundamentally fueled by jealousy. As another *midrash* points out, the path from the relatively light sin of eating the forbidden fruit leads—inexorably—to the much more serious violation of life itself.

The midrashic concern, then, is with humankind, not with the serpent, who becomes a dramatic device through which the ethos finds expression. The moral seems to be that sin will not merely fail at its purpose; it will also deprive the person of his very humanity, the status for which he has been created. Man yearning to be "as God" is not judged kindly. And, in the talmudic, humanized refraction of this teaching, it is jealousy per se that destroys—there is no need for an external, punishing deity.

On another level, suggested by both the midrashic language ("the serpent set its eyes on that which was not proper for it; what it sought was not granted and what it possessed was taken from it") and the example of adulterous behavior, sin consists of striving to take (or to become) what is beyond yours by right. One wonders, then, whether the midrashic message is not social as well as interpersonal? Perhaps the individual is being warned not to reach beyond his social status? To stay in his place? Let us recall, however, that in all the cases cited—from the serpent on—the individuals are rebelling against the limits of their God-given status or possessions; even the adulterous wife, who perhaps has not received her husband by divine agency (or has she?), is rejecting divine norms. But I do not recall that the rabbinic tradition regards social station, occupation, and the like to be a divine bestowal or even a vocation.

TRAGIC KNOWLEDGE

"Now the serpent was more subtle . . ." (Genesis
3:1). For in much wisdom is much anger, and he that
increaseth knowledge increaseth sorrow (Ecclesiastes
1:18): Because man increases his wisdom he increases
anger against himself, and because he increases his
knowledge he adds to his sorrow. Solomon said:
Because I have multiplied wisdom to myself I multiplied anger against myself, and because I increased
my knowledge I increased my sorrows. Did you ever
hear anybody say: "This ass went out and caught the
sun [i.e., ague], or caught a fever"? And where is
suffering prevalent? With human beings. Rabbi said:
A scholar does not require a warning. R. Johanan
said: It is like the fine linen garments which come from
Beth Shean: if they are even slightly blackened they
are ruined; but as for the [coarse] linen garments
which come from Arbel, what is their value altogether? R. Ishmael taught: According to the camel, so
is its load. It often happens that two people enter a
tavern; one orders, "Bring me roast meat, white

*bread, and good wine," while the other orders, "Bring
me bread and beets": the former eats and suffers
afterwards, while the latter eats and does not suffer.
Thus, human ills weigh heavily up upon one but not
upon the other. It was taught in R. Meir's name:
According to the greatness of the serpent so was his
downfall: because he was "More subtle than all," he
was* more cursed than all *(Genesis 3:14).*

"Now the serpent was more subtle than any beast
*of the field." R. Hoshaya the Elder said: He stood out
distinguished [erect] like a reed, and he had feet. R.
Jeremiah b. Eleazar said: He was an unbeliever. R.
Simeon b. Eleazar said: He was like a camel. He
deprived the world of much good, for had this not
happened, one could have sent his merchandise
through him, and he would have gone and returned.*

—*Genesis Rabbah* 19:1

The *midrash* seems to hit the nail right on the head by connecting
Ecclesiastes 1:18 to Eden. ". . . he that increaseth knowledge
increaseth sorrow" is a virtual commentary on the story of Adam
and Eve, who, eating of the Tree of Knowledge, discover how
much sorrow they then inherit. It is a double legacy: first, they
are cursed by God, but, having become endowed with "knowledge," they will also live with the consciousness of the curses and
their terrors. Ecclesiastes lifts the Genesis narrative out of its
seemingly well-defined time frame, generalizes its truth, and even
expands it. He or she who "increases" knowledge, Ecclesiastes
tells us, repeats the sin of our forefathers and will experience its
burden.

∞

Genesis Rabbah 19:1 is not particularly striking at first glance. It adds its homely exemplars to the unsettling truth of Ecclesiastes, but there seems to be little else. One characteristic perspective does emerge, though. The anger and sorrow produced by wisdom and knowledge are not the anguish brought on by intellectual doubt, the confusion born of skepticism, or the resignation of those who "cannot stand too much reality." The focus is not subjective. Rather, according to the *midrash*, Solomon speaks of the objective guilt—and punishment—brought by additional knowledge, for responsibility is the fundamental outcome of knowledge. Knowledge, for the *midrash*, is knowledge of the Torah and its laws, and the person who knows these is more responsible than the person who is ignorant of them.

Solomon himself is not only "the wisest of all men." In some midrashic traditions, he is the paradigm of a man who sins because of his knowledge of the Law, because he assumes that by knowing—and respecting—the purpose of the Law, he need not observe its particulars. But any scholar, even one with all good intentions, "does not require warning" to be judged culpable; he is forewarned by virtue of his knowledge. Even beyond that: more is rightfully expected of him, and he is therefore blackened by what would hardly stain others. It comes down to a very special kind of *noblesse oblige*. If there is anguish, it is the anguish of the person who knows fully well what is required of him, and who understands how far he has fallen from that standard.

∞

Perhaps this reading diminishes the force of the biblical ". . . in much wisdom is much anger" for most moderns, who appreciate subjective states much more than objective ones. Indeed, I am not at all sure that even many traditionalists wouldn't find the midrashic reading somewhat constricting, squeezing the life out of Ecclesiastes by turning an existential assertion into a virtually legalistic claim or, at most, a confession within the normative life.

Be this as it may, we ought also to consider the *position* of this *midrash*, that is to say, the meaning that is implied by its context. But discovering the true context is no simple matter. R. Meir taught, the Midrash concludes, that "according to the greatness of the serpent so was his downfall," because he was "more subtle than all," he was "more cursed than all." It would seem, then, that the serpent is another case of knowledge—for in that lay his "greatness"—leading to greater guilt and, therefore, to proportionate punishment. From the perspective of literary history, the entire *midrash* would then be, first, a comment on Ecclesiastes 1:18. It was appended to Genesis' description of the serpent as being wiser than all the other creatures—where we find it—simply because it concluded with R. Meir's comment about the serpent, which took Genesis 3:1 as its point of departure (a familiar midrashic technique). Or, if that is not enough to explain the presence of this *midrash* in an exposition of Genesis, we can read it as an introduction to the sin of eating of the Tree of Knowledge of Good and Evil. In that case, the true subjects of the *midrash* are Adam and Eve, humankind.

But this reading takes the easy way out. If we seriously consider the *midrash* as it presents itself to us, its primary topic is Genesis 3:1, *which describes the serpent,* not Adam and Eve. In its present position, then, the discussion of Ecclesiastes' "in much wisdom is much anger" focuses on the serpent, not on humankind. And, rather than the serpent being an exemplar of the human situation, the human cases are, in fact (though superficially), later concretizations of the truth first embodied in the serpent—as R. Meir hinted.

All of this reinforces the original biblical puzzle, deepening it as well. The serpent now not only testifies to an evil that was present before human sin; it also possessed wisdom before humankind ate of the forbidden Tree of Knowledge. (Is it the same knowledge that Adam and Eve would gain by their eating? Or wisdom of a different sort?) Furthermore, the human and cultural analogies cited in the rest of the *midrash* (now appended to Genesis 3:1), beginning with Solomon, suggest that the serpent's wisdom was originally destined for constructive purposes. (Incidentally, this very motif is, in fact, explicit in other midrashic traditions.)

Thus, the image of the serpent changes, becoming complex and ambiguous. Rather than representing pure evil, the serpent is a tragic figure whose downfall matches its stature. It is not merely a matter of depriving the serpent of "what was his" because he reached beyond his proper station; rather, God takes a correct measure of the serpent's persona and responds accordingly. His anger and revenge are directed not at simple sin, but at the corruption of a high destiny. Once again, the serpent is a paradigm of human fate.

Are we exaggerating? Perhaps. Even the "greatness" of which R. Meir speaks is relative, after all, to that of the other creatures of the field. But the midrashic exposition of Ecclesiastes 1:18 makes itself felt. The serpent is the first paradigm of "knowledge [which] increases sorrow." Perhaps, indeed, those who most acutely felt the accusation embodied in "in much wisdom is much anger"—the rabbis and their students, those who "do not require warning"—felt that their sins were those of the serpent, and not those of the more innocent Adam and Eve? Even "human ills" weigh only upon he who eats roast meat and white bread. So the presence of the serpent in the Eden story serves to reinforce the guilt and heighten the self-accusation of the rabbinic authors of the *midrash*. The serpent is not merely a dramatic device for exploring commonplace human sin; it has become a type of spirituality gone wrong and thus a model for rabbinic identification.

∽

But have we exaggerated? Overreacted to a casual editorial joining of *midrash* to Scripture? Consider the following:

> Rabbi said: If the serpent had not been cursed . . .
> man would have introduced him into use instead
> of the horse, mule, and donkey, and he would have
> carried manure for man to the gardens and
> orchards.
> R. Simeon ben Elazar said . . . a man would
> have bought two serpents for himself and would
> have sent one to the north and one to the south,
> and in thirty days they would have brought him
> silver and gold. (*Fathers According to R. Nathan*,
> version B, chapter 1, trans. A. Saldarini [Leiden
> 1975], p. 32)

I have long been puzzled by these statements and others like them. What are they trying to say about the serpent? Why say it?

I would suggest, in the light of our prior discussion, that these comments are very precisely—and comically—directed at those who do, in fact, overemphasize the serpent's "greatness." R. Meir is not necessarily one of those teachers, although the chronology would fit. We also know of sectarian, gnostic groups for whom the serpent was hero, not villain, a shining creature who fought the Lord. This *midrash* paints the serpent as "great," but in a rather humiliating sense. He is talented and able and would have done much better at hauling manure than the animals who now do the job; he would also have made the ideal business agent.

Perhaps, indeed, the serpent is better off cursed? He has lost much, but he need not toil for his human masters! Better, perhaps, to be hated by humanity than exploited by it.

ABSENT ADAM

> *"And the woman said unto the serpent: of the fruit of the trees of the garden we may eat" (Genesis 3:2). Now where was Adam during this conversation? Abba Halfon b. Koriah said: He had engaged in sexual intercourse and then fallen asleep. The Rabbis said: He [God] took him and led him all around the world, telling him: "Here is a place fit for planting [trees], here is a place fit for sowing [cereals]." Thus it is written, Through a land that no man passed through, and where no man (adam) dwelt (Jeremiah 2:6): that is, Adam had not dwelt there.*

> —*Genesis Rabbah* 19:3a

It is possible, from a purely formal point of view, to imagine that the explicit midrashic question is really the last in a series of questions: First, why did the serpent talk to Eve? Wouldn't he have spoken, rather, with Adam? If he didn't, it must have been because Adam was not available. And so, the question explicitly asked: Where was Adam? It is not likely, though, that this was the

21

question's intention. The thrust of the entire biblical account, and even more so that of the *midrash*, is that the serpent most deliberately *chose* to speak with Eve, the woman; she was not a substitute for an unavailable Adam. The reason for this preference may lie in the sexual hum running just below the surface of the entire episode, or it may be found in the more chauvinistic assumption of feminine gullibility (as another *midrash* put it, ". . . I cannot trip up Adam, I shall go and trip up Eve"). Indeed, the midrashic question is paternalistic in its essence. But, for whatever reason, the *midrash* could not have thought that the serpent's target of choice would have been Adam. Far from representing cosmic evil, the serpent chose to talk with Eve because he was nothing more than a scoundrel.

The midrashic certainty that Adam was not present during the conversation is based, rather, on the assumption that Adam should have protected Eve from the serpent's suggestions, or, more pragmatically, that the serpent would never have dared approach her with them if Adam was in the neighborhood—or perhaps he would not have dared approach her at all, for that matter. That is the reason for the questioner's wonder: "Now where was Adam . . . ?" The atmosphere is thoroughly bourgeoise, and the roles are fully defined and functioning.

The midrashic replies display the domestic, bourgeoise image to the fullest. Is a comic message intended? The *midrash* does not usually engage in the genre, but who knows? Adam, we are told, was fully the male partner, the normal husband—with all of his characteristics and responsibilities. As different as the two midrashic replies are, they at least have that in common: Adam, in both instances, performs as a good husband should.

ଏବ

Abba Halfon returns us to the sexual motif found in Genesis 18:6. Adam and Eve made love—once again, sexual behavior is emphatically not a result of eating the forbidden fruit—and, in typical male fashion, Adam has fallen asleep. Perhaps there is a hint that though Adam had been sexually satisfied, Eve had not. Eve has been left awake and alone—but, obviously, not quite. The serpent has been hovering in the vicinity for the duration; he was first stimulated by the pair at love, and he remained during Adam's slumber. Envisioning the scene, it is difficult not to see in the serpent's conversation with Eve at this juncture, a symbolic replacing of Adam—which, as we recall, was his ultimate goal. Perhaps, indeed, the serpent's conversation with Eve is a more serious and meaningful communication than the physical, sexual connection with Adam. The serpent, in any case, does not attempt to seduce Eve sexually. He takes a longer view.

None of this, however, is the major point of the *midrash*, which is to relate to Adam's role. Now, if it is Adam's duty to protect Eve, he has failed, somewhat ridiculously. This may say something about the midrashic view of sex, or of male behavior therein; it may be a way of shifting more of the blame to Adam; or it may only be the solution to the practical dilemma posed by the original question. It may even be all of these. The picture of the serpent talking with Eve while Adam is asleep nearby does, in any case, provide an amusing tableux.

∾

The picture drawn by the Rabbis is less entertaining but more provocative. (Here, too, an investigation of the literary history of the motif concerned may reveal a theme wrenched out of its original context and changed drastically thereby; but, here again, we shall concern ourselves only with the text as it presents itself to us.) Adam is not present to protect Eve. Again, we should imagine the serpent stalking his prey watchfully, waiting until it is most vulnerable. He will enter at that most obvious hour, when the husband is away at work. Eve will not wonder why the serpent arrives just then; nor will she suggest that he return when her husband is home so that he, too, can listen.

Yet, despite the piquancy of this elaboration, the *midrash* is provocative for another reason and in a different direction. For the Rabbis now introduce a fourth character: God. God took Adam away from Eve, making him an undoubtedly irresistible offer (". . . led him all around the world"). Is God partly responsible then, even at this early stage, for what will happen? Is this tour a deliberate tactical diversion, God co-operating with his creature, the serpent, so as to leave Eve outside Adam's protective shield? Did He know to what He was exposing her?

Moreover, why does God take Adam *all around the world*? Adam, to the best of both his knowledge and ours, is ensconced in the Garden of Eden and does not expect to be driven from it. God seems to be preparing him for a future outside the Garden, a future of work, if not toil. It almost seems as if they both understand that life in the Garden is temporary, a hiatus. Adam, after all, was created outside the Garden and then placed there (Genesis 2:7–8, 2:15). This already suggests that it is not his natural home. But Adam certainly could not have imagined the conditions under which he would leave the Garden! Perhaps he even thought that "all the world," through which his creator and benefactor so graciously guided him, would merely be an extension of the Garden, which he had also been commanded to "work and to guard" (Genesis 2:15)? Possibly, but the Garden was planted with trees—not with cereals. Adam may have been innocent of all this, but the reader is not—nor was God. God, then, functions at both poles of the story, even joining them in one paradoxical act. Primarily, He enables the sin by drawing Adam away from Eve; but He does this by providing the means through which the sin's immediate result will be overcome. He conspires, in a sense, with both (a knowing) serpent and (an unknowing) Adam at the same time, fashioning a midrashic Möbius strip, as it were.

So God prepares an unsuspecting Adam for his future, giving him tools, knowledge, and education. This is a sadder God, but also a practical one. Perhaps He knows that after the sin, it will not be so easy to reach Adam. He will have to punish Adam and Eve, drive them out of the Garden. There will be anger, recrimination. Now is a time when advice can be easily given and naturally accepted; Adam believes he is simply being introduced to more divine bountifulness. A younger Adam and God can enjoy visiting the shining world together.

So while the serpent talks with Eve, God walks with Adam. Eve's conversation paves the way for the (inexorable?) exile; Adam's journey prepares the ground for life outside the Garden.

WHEN A FENCE IS TOO HIGH: ADAM AND AUTHORITY

"But of the fruit of the tree which is in the midst of the garden, God hath said: Ye shall not eat of it, neither shall ye touch it, lest ye die" (Genesis 3:3). Thus it is written, Add not unto His words, lest He reprove thee, and thou be found a liar *(Proverbs 3:6). R. Hiyya taught: That means that you must not make the fence more than the principal thing, lest it fall and destroy the plants. Thus, the Holy One, blessed be He, had said,* For in the day that thou eatest thereof thou shalt surely die *(Genesis 2:17); whereas she did not say thus, but, "God hath said: Ye shall not eat of it, neither shall ye touch it"; when he [the serpent] saw her thus lying, he took and thrust her against it. "Have you then died?" he said to her; "just as you were not stricken through touching it, so will you not die when you eat it, but* For God doth know that in the day ye eat thereof . . ." (ibid., 5).

—*Genesis Rabbah* 19:3b

The *midrash* before us contains both a narrative and its moral. It is careful *not* to say that the rule is learned *from* the story, and, indeed, the moral is presented *before* the story. Thus, the story exemplifies a rule already known, either from common sense or from the verse in Proverbs. Perhaps the rule should have been known even to Adam (or Eve), who is then blamed for not taking it to heart. It will not do to to ask how Adam can be expected to know this at the very beginning of human history. Common sense already exists. So, too, in a sense, does the Book of Proverbs: for the midrashic sensibility, all of God's revelation—in the broadest sense—is present and available from the beginning, and Moses, Isaiah, and Adam can exchange words, ideas, and experience across time. Adam, moreover, is much more than the First Man for this *midrash*.

∾

The midrashic editor notwithstanding, I shall first study the narrative, which he placed second, not R. Hiyya's moral (which he placed first).

The conversation between Eve and the serpent is an exercise in extremes, a ricochet of radical possibilities. The serpent begins with a question: "Did God really say, You shall not eat of any tree of the garden?" (Temptation, as Bonhoeffer was to point out, begins with a question; but a Jew might answer that the Talmud does, too). Eve must have been startled, perhaps thrown off balance, by the serpent's knowledge of what had been said by God to humankind. But let us remember that she had not heard the command directly from God; it must have been told to her by Adam. And who knows to whom else Adam had spoken? And whom else God had commanded?

Eve replies that she and Adam might eat of all the trees; they simply could not eat or even touch only one single tree. There is exaggeration here; compared to God's original command not to eat of the tree, Eve has added that even touching it is forbidden. The average listener would hear a simple overdramatization of God's words in Eve's, perhaps an elaboration fueled by the serpent's own distortion, a reply thrown out when caught off balance. Eve's major assertion, after all, is that she and Adam were permitted to eat of every single tree—almost. By adding that the tree could not be touched, she was convincing herself, as it were, of its noxious character; the tree was thoroughly and objectively evil, and any contact with it was dangerous. Who, after all, would *want* to *touch* the tree? But the serpent, as the *midrash* tells us, is not an average listener. He takes advantage of Eve's exaggeration and is able to undermine her faith.

Now although Eve is described here as being responsible for the exaggeration, this cannot have been the case. For Eve is terribly disturbed when she sees that she is unscathed after touching the tree, which would not have happened had she invented that ban—she would have known that touching the tree could do no harm. True, she could have been convinced by her own elaboration, or she could have innocently misinterpreted the words of God. But, in the latter case, the narrative would not lead to the moral (as we shall see); the former suggestion is possible, but not terribly plausible. However, our problem is solved in other midrashic versions. These presentations give the incident a slightly different twist, one that can just be tolerated in our text as well.

"Adam," we read elsewhere, "did not . . . speak to Eve the way God had spoken to him. Rather, this is what he said to her: 'But of the fruit of the tree which is in the midst of the garden, God has said, You shall not eat of it, nor shall you touch it.'" *These are Eve's words to the serpent, but this* midrash *claims that they were Adam's words to her as well.* That is to say, Eve, innocent and obedient to the core, unwarily repeated to the serpent what Adam had told her.

This reconstruction makes good, if subtle, textual sense. Eve, as we have pointed out, did not receive God's command directly. She was created, according to the story of Genesis 3, *after* God had commanded Adam; and the midrash assumes that he—and not God—had commanded her. This assumption may reflect the text's silence (it doesn't describe God repeating His command) or rabbinic views of God's reluctance to converse with women; or, it may have been invented to enable the tale and its moral to be told (for the biblical text doesn't describe Adam commanding Eve, either). Either way, the distortion of God's command is Adam's work, motivated either by arrogant paternalism or simple distrust.

Why would Adam not give God's command to Eve as it had been given to him? The *midrash* does not say, but it seems likely that he simply did not trust her. If she could get close to the tree, he thought, she just might be attracted by its fruits. . . . Better to keep her at arm's length, at least. Ironically, then, Eve displays perfect obedience and good faith in her conversation with the serpent—and it is this that destroys her. Rather than being to blame for Adam's fate, she is a victim of his lack of trust in her. In this reading, Eve's sin is not a product of her initial openness to the serpent, its claims about God and her potential to be "as Him," or the attractiveness of the tree. She is first betrayed by Adam.

Since she had no reason to suspect Adam of distorting God's command, Eve's only conclusion can be the serpent's. God's entire command, which has been mediated to her by Adam, is now suspect; His insistence that she and Adam not eat of the tree, she must think, is not meant to protect them but rather to deprive them of a status He jealously guards for Himself. God, He Who commanded them, has lied—for His own purposes. Why not eat of the tree and achieve what is rightfully theirs?

The serpent convinces Eve that touching the tree brings no harm (and that she can also eat of it in full confidence) by pushing her against its trunk. This demonstration is instructive. For one thing, it brings the serpent into physical contact with Eve, contact that is forced upon her: this would not go easily in the traditional culture of the *midrash*. She was, it is true, "passing near the tree" when the serpent pushed her, and one can wonder whether she invited his thrust, ever so discretely. But this, I think, is going too far. Nor is that all.

If Eve was indeed convinced by the serpent's maneuver, her conception of the evil tree must have been primitive. For, even though she was forced to touch the tree (we can well imagine that, fearful as she undoubtedly was, she did not cooperate!), she nevertheless expects to be punished, struck dead. She was fully surprised to be spared after coming into contact with the tree, which was, therefore, an object of magical power, not an instrument to prove mature devotion. The crudity of the serpent's technique was matched by the grossness of Eve's response. To be fair, I suppose, one could urge that this response was instinctive; yet Eve did not seem to rethink this instinctive reaction, if that is what it was.

A more sophisticated—and gallant—serpent would have touched the tree himself (which is what he does in yet another midrashic version). True, having Eve come into contact with the tree herself carries with it the force of firsthand physical experience. But much can be gained by the serpent willfully touching the tree himself as she watches. This act would be fully volitional, and would deserve to be punished—if the divine warning were true; this, then, was a meaningful test of God's word. Certainly, it is fair to assume that the ban on the tree applied to all creatures—serpents no less than humans. And, by daring to

touch the tree himself, the serpent would prove his commitment
to Eve, his concern for her destiny. He would even risk his own
life to demonstrate that he spoke only truth to her.

The midrashic narrative creates and then fills a textual gap; it
also responds to an anomaly in the text itself (". . . nor touch
it"). If we have understood its tale correctly, it adds an interesting
dimension to the human relationship of Adam and Eve and may
even redress the balance of guilt. But it has also made a statement
about the pedagogy of normative loyalty and the way it can be
destroyed, and about the use and abuse of authority. For Adam
mediates the word of God to Eve; his decision to make that word
more severe than it actually was, set in motion a train of events
that destroyed her fundamental commitment to that word itself.
Done perhaps for a fine motive (or perhaps not: Adam must have
assumed that Eve was less to be trusted than he himself was by
God!)—nevertheless, it was a mistake.

This reading may seem remote from the midrashic tale, set in
primeval Eden, but it is very relevant to the rabbinic authors of
midrash. They saw themselves as mediators of God's word to
Israel, responsible for both transmitting the Law and educating
the people in its observance. On this broader phenomenological
level, the serpent's maneuver is merely a symbolic acting-out of
the dynamic inherent in normative over-kill, one that remains a
constant in every generation. This, of course, is the moral
articulated by R. Hiyya in the first section of our *midrash*, a moral
addressed very specifically to the Rabbis themselves.

ᔏ

R. Hiyya explicitly addresses the scriptural warning of Proverbs
30:6: "Add not unto His words, lest He reprove thee, and thou be
found a liar." Although we shall focus on the lesson R. Hiyya
teaches rabbinic legislators, it is clear that R. Hiyya himself was

also attempting to draw the sting of a very embarrassing verse. For if one was not to add *anything* to the divine Law (as Deuteronomy 13:1 insisted, as well) then the rabbinic enterprise—with its manifold extensions of that Law, its new pieces of legislation, its safeguarding "fences"—was profoundly illegitimate, inviting the reproof of God Himself. Thus, R. Hiyya, although warning his rabbinic contemporaries, was in effect reinterpreting Proverbs 30:1. It does not, he argues, reject all new legislation, only the kind that "makes the fence more than the principal thing." The point of the verse, then, was to guide the rabbinic legislator, not to eliminate him.

But this was probably R. Hiyya's primary purpose as well. Talmudic culture had long ago found the *modus vivendi* between the biblical passages mandating absolute fealty to scriptural religion, on the one hand, and the rabbinic vocation of adding and subtracting, on the other. If Deuteronomy 13:1 could be accommodated, Proverbs 30:1 could be, too. Indeed, this entire issue, in a sense, was (and has remained) theoretical, challenging rabbinic thinkers to provide an abstract justification for that which had been done for centuries. The concrete questions were (and have remained): What to legislate? What are the limits? How to balance the assumed need to add rigor and specificity to the biblical Law with the concern lest the Law collapse of its own weight? R. Hiyya's advice was directed to those problems, which each generation answers anew as it grapples with its own normative dilemmas and solutions.

R. Hiyya does not offer a formulaic solution, of course; but his message is clear, as he stresses the limits that ought to be placed on rabbinic legislation of the kind that adds to biblical norms. Others had said the same thing: "R. Yose said, 'Better a standing fence of ten handbreadths, than one of a hundred cubits that falls down.'" The higher fence apparently offers greater protection, but it also collapses more easily under its own weight or from prevailing winds. R. Hiyya's own simile is less clear; but his point also seems to be that too high a fence is worse than none. That, after all, is what the story of Adam and Eve proved. One need merely substitute the workings of the psyche and will for the serpent's manipulation of Eve on this very point. And, by addressing Proverbs 30:1, R. Hiyya has scriptural warrant for his warning: God's reproof is now directed precisely at those who "add to His words" in the sense just explicated, "who make the fence more than the principal thing." Indeed, R. Hiyya probably attached his teaching to Proverbs 30:1 rather than to Deuteronomy 13:1, in order to gain divine sanction for his admonition.

Rabbinic legislators could be self-conscious about their task and its responsibilities, aware of the complexity and delicacy of legal and spiritual cost–benefit analysis. R. Hiyya implies that mistakes were sometimes made, that good intentions backfired. He understood—and condemned—the facile assumption that greater severity promised greater control, or, more success in assuring obedience.

One ought to note, finally, that there is a slight discrepancy between the midrashic narrative about Adam and Eve and the moral attached to it by R. Hiyya and others. Adam had misinformed Eve; he had fooled her into thinking that God's command had included the notion that the tree could not be touched. But the rabbinic "fence" admits its human origins; it clearly distinguishes between the scriptural norm and the rabbinic addition. Perhaps, though, this distinction was not always so clear—either in practice or in theory. Perhaps even rabbinic legislation was presented, or, in good faith, understood to be an organic extension of the divine Law? And perhaps many Jews considered their rabbis to be spokesmen for God? The loyal Jew is expected to be as faithful to rabbinic law as to the divine Torah, and the psychological mechanisms that enable this commitment must exist, too.

MYTH: THE SERPENT'S LIE

R. Joshua of Siknin said, in R. Levi's name: He [the serpent] began speaking slander of his Creator, saying, "Of this tree did He eat and then create the world; hence He orders you, ye shall not eat thereof, so that you may not create other worlds, for every person hates his fellow craftsmen." R. Judah b. R. Simon said: He argued: "Whatever was created after its companion dominates it. Thus: heaven was created on the first day and the firmament on the second: does it not bear its weight? The firmament was created on the second and herbs on the third: do they not interrupt its waters? Herbs were created on the third day and the luminaries on the fourth; the luminaries on the fourth and the birds on the fifth." R. Judah b. R. Simon said: The ziz is a clean bird, and when it flies, it obscures the orb of the sun. "Now you were created after everything in order to rule over everything; make haste and eat before He creates other worlds which will rule over you." Hence it is written, And the woman saw that

> it was good . . . *(Genesis 3:6): she saw [how*
> *plausible were] the words of the serpent.*
>
> —*Genesis Rabbah* 19:4

R. Levi and R. Judah b. R. Simon place different arguments in the
serpent's mouth, but there are also elements in common. For
both of them, the magical tree—for the tree is clearly magical if
one ascribes to it the powers the serpent does—grants the power
to participate in the act of creation, indeed, to control it. And this
is what the serpent offers humanity by proposing. "You shall be
as God." This concrete offer enticed humankind much more than
the abstract "knowledge of good and evil." True, this potential is
not mentioned in the Bible; but perhaps the *midrash* atomized
Scripture: "You shall be as gods"—with the power to create, in
addition to "knowing good and evil." Let us recall, too, with
Buber, that the creation of humankind in the "image of God"
immediately encourages—indeed, obliges—human imitation of
God. This image, moreover, probably lies in the ability to
dominate much of the created world. "Let us make man in our
image, after our likeness. They shall rule the fish of the sea, the
birds of the sky, the cattle, the whole earth . . ." (Genesis 1:26).
The distance from dominion to creation is not far.

The serpent also called up the possibility of "other worlds," a
fantasy that perhaps engaged the rabbinic imagination no less
than it does our own. The *midrash* elsewhere plays with the
possibility of other worlds, arguing that no other imagined world
would have been as successful as this one ("no one can say: 'were
I to have three eyes or three hands or three feet, or were I to walk
on my head, or were my head to point backwards, how good it
would be . . .'") or telling that God created many worlds and
destroyed them before He made this one, which He approved of

and which He therefore preserved. In both these examples, the present creation is indeed declared the best of worlds. The serpent's tactic, though, is to suggest that other worlds—better ones or worse—are possible. Is the possibility of a different world so powerful an option? Or, rather, is it the power to control the act of creation that humankind cannot resist?

ॐ

R. Levi has the serpent slander God (Who is *his* creator as well), making him not only a liar but also an ingrate—on two counts, the moral and the theological. First, he develops the biblical suggestion that God is jealous of His creatures and so withholds from them abilities that would close the gap between He and they—first, the "knowledge of good and evil," and now, the ability to create, to be a "fellow craftsman" with the Lord Himself. And by stating that God gets the power to create by eating of the tree, the serpent denies the basic monotheistic belief that God is truly supreme and is not dependent on other beings or objects.

The assertion that God ate of "this tree and then creat[ed] the world" is *mythos*, one that may well be rooted in the sectarian-gnostic reality of rabbinic times or in even more ancient pagan times. But it can also be rendered in more general terms. In this scheme, God is not the creator of all, including the Tree of Knowledge. Rather, *it* created Him, for it was by His eating of its fruits that He gained the power to be God. And, the logic continues, if it created Him, it can create you as well, make of you creators. In a sense, this is not radically different from the underlying theme of the biblical narrative; there, too, "you will be as God, knowing good and evil" if you eat of the Tree, so it is apparently the Tree that gives—even to God—that knowledge. But in the Bible, the serpent only makes a trace of a suggestion. R. Levi has him paint a physical picture, describing for Eve how

God, too, "ate" of the fruit. Naturally, since Eve ought to realize that God was the serpent's creator as well as hers—indeed, he does not contest that fact—she ought also to realize that the serpent has no way of knowing what God did or did not do before creation and that, consequently, he must be lying.

While the story of God eating, as it were, from the Tree of Knowledge outrages the Jewish ear, it is not really the central fact for Adam and Eve, merely a necessary detail in the serpent's case. They are truly seduced by the possibility that they, too, can "create other worlds," transforming themselves in the process from creatures to creators. These ambitions are, perhaps, not an entirely bad thing. As Buber points out, man was created "in the image of God," and so his striving to become "as God," to concretize the image—though not to supplant its author—may even be seen as humanity's commanded destiny. Similarly, with the human thrust to imitate the divine creator by creating other worlds. The rabbinic ethos frequently urges *imitatio dei*, at least of His moral characteristics, so why not "Just as He creates, so, too, should you create"? Why are these ambitions, sins? Would a more technological age be more sympathetic to the serpent's invitation? But Buber also points to the basic mistake, which was to assume that one could participate in the divine image by eating of the fruit of a tree. Such participation requires other substantive achievements.

The same is true of our *midrash*. In the serpent's suggestion, humankind is brought to near-divine status by reducing God to human dimensions. The mythological slander, "of this tree did He eat and then create the world," is, then, of the essence. (Indeed, this mythic explanation of creativity denigrates the creative individual, as well as God.) Human creativity, moreover, is characterized as an assault upon God, who perceives it as a threat to his prerogative—"every person hates his fellow crafts-man"—rather than as a form of participation in the divine bountifulness. It is difficult to claim that the *midrash* would have been sympathetic to the basic notion that humanity is charged with "creating worlds"; this idea may involve a thoroughly modern value. Yet it is paradoxically clear that the serpent's heresy lay not in promising this power to humankind, but rather in his assumption that it could be gained only if God was first destroyed. Creativity had to be rendered satanic before it could be offered to humanity.

The irony of Eve's seduction then lies in the fact that (as Warren Harvey has pointed out) the serpent offers humanity what we already possess, intrinsically. If created "in the image," we are not only possessed of the ability to create, but we are charged to do so.

∾

According to R. Judah b. R. Simon, the serpent did not offer Adam and Eve the power to create. Rather, he offered them the ability to prevent God from creating new worlds. Yet, despite the absence of the mythic image of R. Levi's *midrash* ("of this tree did He eat . . ."), the serpent of this *midrash* makes an equally mythic proposal: That although God does not derive the power to create from nature itself, nature can nevertheless prevent Him from further creation, as when Adam and Eve eat of the tree. The exact dynamics of this process are none too clear, but it is apparent that he who eats of the tree can freeze creation, so that it can go no further.

The significant difference between these two stories lies, then, not on the theological level but on the anthropological one. The point concerns what each one says about man, not what each one says about God. For R. Levi, humankind is tempted by the possibility of becoming master creators; we are moved even to sin by intimations of grandeur. For R. Judah b. R. Simon, though, Adam and Eve are dominated by fear and egotism.

For R. Judah, humankind desires to freeze creation in its tracks because, above all, it fears loss of status and prerogative. By responding to the serpent, Adam and Eve accept his description of their own function: "you were created . . . in order to rule over everything." Again, the key term is *power*—the power to dominate. That is the obverse of the need to prevent progress, to speak in anachronistic terms. In this perspective, the developmental pattern of creation does not express growth and mutuality, but exploitation, as each new stage dominates that which came before. As is common, Adam and Eve assume the permanence of their own prerogative—it is even divinely mandated ("you were created in order . . .")—though they know full well that they must sin in order to prevent God from creating what they fear may well replace them. Or, to draw on the familial metaphor, humankind is convinced of God's special love but is also certain ("make haste . . .") that He will shortly have a different favorite, a new baby.

R. Judah's *midrash* indirectly addresses another, if somewhat trivial, question, a conundrum classically raised by the biblical story itself. Shouldn't Eve ask the serpent: "Why don't you eat of the tree yourself? If the fruit is so good and useful, and God's threat so empty . . ." It is possible to suggest numerous ripostes to this query, both of the kind that the serpent himself could have offered Eve, and of the kind that he could not—those which would take us deeper into her situation and her relationship with the serpent. Our *midrash* provides its own solution, intended or not. The serpent could not eat of the tree because it was too late; it had missed its chance. Once humankind had been created, the serpent's master was already in existence.

Ironically, the achievement of the serpent disproves the simplistic thesis he had foisted on Adam and Eve. Being himself of a lower status than humankind, he proves that the lower form can indeed dominate the higher, that that which came later does not necessarily control that which came earlier. The serpent controlled Eve, after all, not the reverse. However, seen in a less moralistic perspective, our story can be read—as story—differently. The serpent knows that although he was created "the most subtle of all the creatures of the field," he has been superceded. Humankind does exist now, and it is superior. The serpent is taking revenge on God, through His new creatures.

EVE:
THE FEAR AND
THE LONELINESS

"She took of the fruit thereof, and did eat." R. Aibu said, "She squeezed grapes and gave him." R. Simlai said, "She came upon him with her answers all ready, saying to him: 'What think you: that I will die and another Eve will be created for you?'—There is nothing new under the sun *(Ecclesiates 1:9). 'Or do you think that I will die while you remain alone?'"* He created it not a waste, He formed it to be inhabited *(Isaiah 45:18). The Rabbis said: She began weeping and crying over him.*

—*Genesis Rabbah 19:5*

If Eve received God's command not to eat of the fruit from Adam, Adam received the fruit itself from Eve. I do not know if some ironic form of tit-for-tat isn't operating here, but Adam taking the fruit from Eve is a matter for some thought. The transaction sounds very smooth and, in the New JPS translation, even pedestrian: "She took of its fruit and ate. She also gave some to her husband and he ate." Does he know the source of the fruit he is given? And if he does, why does he eat it? Is he, too, convinced by the serpent's insinuations, passed on to him by Eve? Suggestively, the Bible reports no conversation between husband and wife; the scene is strangely dreamlike. Or does Adam automatically eat whatever his wife puts before him, in a typical husbandly fashion? Yet he is punished for eating, along with her, so perhaps we ought to assume that he knew what he ate and did so consciously. Perhaps, too, Adam, being responsible for his garden, naturally identified its fruit—which leaves all the more open the question of why he so calmly ate. In any case, it seems obvious that Eve, ever the dutiful and considerate wife ("a fitting helper"), gives Adam the fruit so that he may share in the transformation that she has been promised. Adam, later on, also describes himself as eating out of a virtual sense of duty (as he indirectly blames the Lord for all his troubles): "The woman you put at my side—she gave me of the tree, and I ate" (Genesis 3:12).

Nevertheless, if the Bible says nothing about Eve discussing the fruit with her husband when it tells the story, it will soon hint that Eve was not silent. "Because you listened to your wife's voice and ate of the tree . . ." (Genesis 3:17) is the way a literal translation of God's accusation would read. So Eve, it appears, did speak to Adam about the fruit—although what she said remains an enigma. And even though he is not eager to admit it and attempts to foist on the Lord a version less incriminating to himself, Adam chose to listen. (The Bible frequently provides new details, sometimes quite meaningful, at later points in its narrative; see, for example, the description of Joseph pleading with his brothers, in Genesis 42:21, which is lacking in the Genesis 37 narrative of Joseph's sale. None of these aspects of the story escaped the *midrash*.

The biblical description suggests that Eve gave Adam the fruit naturally, innocently, and in the spirit of pure sharing. It is only after they have eaten together (in Genesis 3:6) that "the eyes of both of them were opened and they perceived that they were naked" (Genesis 3:7). Thus, Eve's eyes are opened, as it were, after she has shared the fruit with Adam; the perception of nakedness and shame will be mutual. She is not aware of the disaster she will cause, before she gives Adam the fruit to eat, nor would she assume that she was doing the wrong thing, unless doubt arose immediately when she herself ate. The point that was left vague in the Bible relates to what Eve said, assuming that the statement "you listened to the voice of your wife" must be taken literally and that it means hearing her speak, rather than following her directive or initiative—which is what Adam had implied. Did Eve tell him where the fruit came from? Did she repeat the arguments of the serpent—or did she simply pass him the fruit to eat? Was she so convinced by the serpent that all creation was swept aside, or did some apprehension still remain?

Our *midrash*—and the midrashic tradition as a whole, in fact—interprets Eve's feeding of Adam very idiosyncratically. Despite the very different impression left by the biblical narrative, the *midrash* tells us that Eve knew full well, immediately upon her own taking of the fruit, that she did wrong. *Her* eyes were opened, apparently, then and there. She knew, of course, that she had survived, but she certainly feared that she would die momentarily. (In one midrashic account, she even sees the angel of death approaching her *before* she eats—but she eats nevertheless.) Thus, the midrashic tradition has Eve giving Adam the fruit deliberately, knowing that she is leading him to sin and possibly death and, indeed, possibly intending these results. We are in the presence of a radical reinterpretation of the biblical story.

Nor does Eve silently or casually hand Adam the fruit; she must convince him to eat. So he knows that she has eaten and sinned, and he is not inclined to follow her blindly. For the *midrash*, it is a moment of honesty, at least compared to the gentle, dreamy dissembling, the ambiguities suggested by the Bible. The ensuing scene (in any of its midrashic versions) finds the pair vigorously in crisis, a crisis resolved by Adam agreeing to eat the fruit, which is now not only an act directed at God and His command. It is—perhaps primarily—a gesture made by Adam toward Eve, a conscious sharing of their mutual fate.

∽

All of this is true for the last two sections of our *midrash*, according to which Eve either attempted rational argument with Adam, or simply overpowered him emotionally. In either case, the *midrash* attempts to "explain" why Adam ate the fruit that Eve offered him, knowing the risk he ran. But what is behind the statement that "she squeezed grapes and gave him"?

It may be that R. Aibu's comment has a different point of departure altogether. The Bible also keeps silent, after all, about the identity of the fruit eaten by Adam and Eve, a strange silence that adds to the enigma of the entire narrative (though some *midrashim* find ethical reasons for this nondisclosure). Different rabbis have their suggestions—the fig, wheat, or grapes are all named. R. Aibu defends the position that the fruit was the grape, because it fits the odd biblical phraseology: Eve takes "*of* the fruit," not "the fruit" itself, thus hinting that she first took something out of the fruit—its juice, the wine of the grape.

R. Aibu would then not be commenting on Eve's success in getting Adam to eat of the fruit; he would be participating in another discussion altogether, one similarly set in motion by the verse in question, which allows identification of the fruit through its description of how it was transmitted to Adam. The fact that Eve gave the wine to Adam is inconsequential. But the matter is not so simple, for if this were the case, why does R. Aibu refer at all to Eve giving the wine to Adam? His point, after all, is simply to identify the fruit of which Eve herself ate, and this point could be made without saying anything about what she gave Adam, or the manner in which she gave it. R. Aibu's comment suggests, moreover, that she did not squeeze the grape when she herself ate of it! R. Aibu does seem to touch, then, on the basic issue of this *midrash* as a whole: Why does Adam eat of the fruit?

Is R. Aibu suggesting that Eve fooled Adam, by not giving him the grape, which he would have recognized as coming from the forbidden tree, but rather its wine? Why is he guilty then—for allowing himself to be outsmarted? Or does wine suggest drunkenness, as though this sin (or sin in general) causes or is set in motion by a loss of control, a surrender to irrationality? On a more pragmatic level, this description suggests Eve's calm, methodical patience: you have to squeeze many grapes before you get enough wine for a cupful.

∾

R. Simlai clearly attacks the problem posed by Adam's willingness to eat the forbidden fruit. Eve did not simply pass it on to an unsuspecting Adam; and, knowing as he was, he wasn't initially eager to eat. She convinced him, in a veritable flurry of defensive arguments and learned citations. Her explicit point was that even as matters stood, she was not going to die. God had created humankind in order to populate the world, and since no new woman would be created if she were to die, her death would be unthinkable—even, or especially, for God. And so, she implied, even if they were both to eat, God's plan required that they stay alive. Ironically, Eve claimed—basing her argument on Scripture—that all of God's promises and plans were sacrosanct, except for his threat to punish the person who ate of the Tree of Knowledge. But Eve did think she was going to die.

Eve revealed her basic fears, which centered more around her relationship with Adam and her jealousy of the continuing life that would be his than on her impending death. She suspected that God would, in fact, create for him a "second Eve," a fear that surfaced elsewhere in the *midrash*. Knowing that she herself was created as his "helper," Eve was apprehensive that this functional need would be met by some other woman. In a different account of our story, this fear was not part of her conversation with Adam, but was an experienced aspect of her sin:

> . . . as soon as Eve ate . . . she saw the angel of death coming toward her. She said: It seems to me as though I am being removed from the world and in the end another woman will be created for Adam instead of me. What shall I do? I will make him eat with me. (*Abot de-Rabbi Nathan*, version B, chap. 1 [trans. A. Saldarini, p. 34])

The characters in the Garden—real or imagined—form a double triangle, then. At first it was Eve, Adam, and his replacement, the serpent. Now, when Eve assumes she is about to die, she constructs the parallel triangle of Adam, Eve, and her own replacement, the second woman. Is Eve's fantasized "other woman" the product of her fear and insecurity? Or is it also a function of her relationship with the serpent, her "other Adam"?

Let us also recall the aggadic tradition that tells that Eve was actually the *second* woman created for Adam. The story is first told by R. Jose to a Roman *matrona*:

> A Roman lady asked R. Jose: Why was woman created . . . in secret?
> —At first He created her for him and he saw her full of discharges and blood; thereupon He

removed her from him and created her for him a
second time.

—I can corroborate your words. It had been
arranged that I should be married to my mother's
brother, but because I was brought up with
him . . . I became plain in his eyes and he went
and married another woman who is not as beau-
tiful as I. (*Genesis Rabbah* 19:7)

The Roman matron (another Eve!) also remains locked in com-
petition with another woman, whom she perceives as her
replacement.

Eve, of course, did not "remember" any of this. But could she
have known or even had an intimation of the fact that she, too,
was not Adam's first woman (assuming that the second woman
created was not identical with the first), that God seemed to have
a commitment to provide Adam with women? Could Adam have
even told her—with any number of possible motives!—that God
had created an earlier helpmeet for him? Such knowledge would
easily transform itself into a fear that Adam was not dependent on
her, that he would be provided with another wife should she be
taken from him. Eve knows, moreover, that Adam once existed
without her, making it all that much easier for her to imagine that
she was not necessarily his eternal companion.

Nor does Eve accuse God alone, or even primarily. "Do you
think" that you will be given "another Eve"? she snarls at Adam;
it is *you* who are already eager to see my replacement. Or,
alternatively, you are happy to be rid of me, preferring to spend
your life alone. Curiously, Eve convinces Adam by undermining
his dreams (to her way of thinking) and returning him to solid
reality.

Contrary to her confident claims, Eve does think she is going
to die. As we see, she has invested much tortured imagination in

picturing what Adam's life will be like after her death. It is less clear what she stands to gain by Adam's death—besides denying him his second Eve or his second bachelorhood. Does she really think that if they both eat, they will both be spared? That God would allow a righteous Adam to populate the world (with a second Eve), but that if he eats, too, God would have no choice but to acquiesce in their continued existence? Perhaps. The other possibility, of course, is that, knowing she is to die, Eve prefers that he die with her.

Adam's eating of the fruit is less transparent. Does the *midrash* describe an Adam who is convinced by his wife? An earlier version of Ahasuerus, that silly king? Or, on the contrary, does Adam see quite through her, to the fear and weakness underneath? Adam, then, eats of the fruit (as Milton has it) for love of this woman, whose greatest terror is that he find satisfaction with a second Eve or alone—without her, in any case. If that is so, the creation of the first human pair is completed only when Adam eats of the forbidden fruit, not in order to betray God but to keep faith with Eve. Or perhaps to keep faith with God, too, He Who had given Eve to him. And God, pretending He did not hear or see, merely accuses, ". . . because you listened to the voice of your wife," you preferred her voice to Mine. Could He be keeping Adam's secret?

∾

The Rabbis tell a different story. Eve does not pass the fruit silently or casually to Adam, but neither does she reason with him or argue it out. Eve is ever the woman—emotional or calculating—whose best weapons are tears and cries. And the Bible does say, "your wife's voice [*kol ishtekha*]," not "your wife's words [*divrei ishtekha*]." The difference in form, moreover, undoubtedly reflects a difference in content.

Now, Eve is clearly not insisting to Adam that God is committed to their survival. On the contrary: she is in a panic, certain that she is to die and somehow expecting that Adam can do something. Yet she is not asking him to save her—but to eat of the fruit with her. It is possible, of course, but even this version retains some content of the previous one and that Eve hoped to manipulate God into preserving her life by forcing Him to choose either between punishing both of them (impossible, if the world was to be populated) or allowing both to escape. However, this seems improbable. Rather, Eve wanted him to eat so that they would face their fate together—so that she might at least have a partner in death, if not in life. Now, however convincing my earlier claim that Adam ate the fruit out of love may have been, here it seems inevitable. Or perhaps "love" is too generous; Adam may simply have been overpowered by his wife's outburst, and the Rabbis may be saying that that, too, is the way of the world. Women neither reason nor cite Scripture—they weep and cry to gain their ends. And men succumb.

IMMORTALITY: THE PHOENIX

"Also" (Genesis 3:6) is an extension; she gave the cattle, beasts, and birds to eat of it. All obeyed her and ate thereof, except a certain bird named hol *[phoenix], as it is written,* Then I said: I shall die with my nest, and I shall multiply my days as the hol—E.V. *"phoenix"* (Job 29:18). *The School of R. Jannai and R. Judan b. R. Simeon differ: The School of R. Jannai maintained: It lives a thousand years, at the end of which a fire issues from its nest and burns it up, yet as much as an egg is left, and it grows new limbs and lives again. R. Judan b. R. Simeon said: It lives a thousand years, at the end of which its body is consumed and its wings drop off, yet as much as an egg is left, whereupon it grows new limbs and lives again.*

—*Genesis Rabbah* 19:5c

If all living creatures—and not only the first humans—ate of the forbidden fruit, then the obvious question "Why do *all* creatures die?" is answered. All creatures die because all creatures ate. One wonders how seriously the Rabbis took this solution, which—

even if taken literally—does not explain why plants and trees wither and fail. The earth, it is true, is "cursed because of you" (Genesis 3:17), but, in context, that apparently refers solely to the loss of its Edenic abundance.

The *midrash* even suggests that the animals did not eat naturally, instinctively, but because they "all listened to her." They, too, are guilty—for without guilt, they would deserve no punishment and could not become mortal. Eve, once again, is she who speaks and convinces, much as with Adam. How did she convince the animals? She could hardly use the arguments she offered Adam. Or, perhaps, she ordered them to eat, and "they obeyed" her? But why did she want them to eat of the fruit? Whence this compelling need that the entire world should sin? In any case, the fundamental interest of the *midrash* is in the guilt of these creatures, not in Eve's role. The possibility that animals can bear guilt is not unusual in the Bible; indeed, the great flood would wipe out all living creatures because "all flesh had corrupted its ways on earth" (Genesis 6:12).

The notion of such guilt is implied by the situation of the phoenix, the only creature that refused to eat of Eve's fruit—and, therefore, that does not die. Clearly, then, the assumption of the *midrash* is that the creature that did not eat, would, in fact, remain immortal; and the phoenix is living proof of this proposition.

But the phoenix is even more—it is living proof that the fruit could have been rejected. All creatures could have resisted Eve, Adam could have refused her, and Eve herself could have spurned the serpent. The action of the phoenix saves freedom of choice.

∾

The phoenix is a mythological creature, and its story was probably absorbed by the *midrash*—or by the Book of Job itself—from international myth. For the Rabbis, myth could be as reliable as scientific observation is for us. The science of the world around them was fully acceptable to *Hazal*, even if its values were not.

Yet with all this said, the process by which myth is absorbed is not quite that flat or unthinking. The phoenix does live forever, in both *midrash* and myth—that much is true. But a reason is given for that situation in the *midrash*. Immortality is not magically inherent in the creature, nor is it bestowed upon the bird at the whim of a god. The phoenix is rewarded with immortality (more precisely, it is not punished with death) because it had the wisdom and the loyalty to obey God's command when the entire world was swayed by appetite. The phoenix is Judaized—not in the trivial sense of becoming a bit player in the biblical story, but because it participates in the deep structure of the biblical ethos, an ethos of responsibility, virtue and guilt, and reward and punishment.

The immortality of the phoenix is peculiar. Rather than living, steady-state, on and on, the phoenix periodically reaches the very abyss of death and virtually ceases to exist. Then, it is renewed. Immortality is given in bursts, as regular spasms. It is not surprising, then, that the phoenix has been interpreted as being both symbol and proof of resurrection. But that is not the purpose of this *midrash*; here, the phoenix is the unique possessor of original, universal immortality, lost by all who live. It is not a creature who prefigures resurrection, which is common to all who die.

If we take the immortality of the phoenix as being emblematic of the fullness of life, then we must conclude that all life, by its very nature and even when possessed of immortality, is a process in which the living being is consumed. One may grow and learn and create in this process, but there is a price to be paid, a price inherent in our very achievement in life. The phoenix is renewed, he is rescued from the final outcome of this process; but he is not spared its basic metabolism. "Only in the Bible . . . does death form part of the natural rhythm of the whole" (R. Josipovici). Perhaps, indeed, our knowledge of this price—and both knowledge and price are the gift of the Tree—is also a basic element in our achievement.

Whatever may have been the literary process that integrated this discussion of the phoenix's immortality with the story of Adam and Eve, that story is now refracted through the tale of the phoenix. Human immortality, too, had it been preserved, would have been rhythmic, a life consumed, lived to completion and then renewed. The metabolism of death is inherent in biology.

The initial creation of Adam from earth requires that the person return to his source (Genesis 3:19), although the promise of immortality would have prevented this ultimate stage (*Mattenot Kehunah*). This is the message of the Tree of Life: placed in the Garden from the beginning—even before the sin takes place—it is the only guarantor of immortality, the only possibility for even unsinning, innocent Adam and Eve to evade death. The Tree of Life affirms both the naturalness of death and the possibility of life. Thus, immortality was not humankind's *natural* fate even then; humanity would simply have been able to periodically rescue itself from the death that was to be its natural fate. Indeed, the Hebrew word for "life" often means "healing." Similarly, eating of the Tree of Knowledge did not itself bring death, which was also there from the beginning. Death comes because humanity is deprived of the restorative Tree of Life. We were created mortal.

THE
FRUIT OF SIN

"And the eyes of them both were opened" (Genesis 3:7). Were they then blind? R. Judan, in the name of R. Johanan b. Zakkai, and R. Berekiah, in the name of R. Akiba, explained it by comparing them to a villager who was passing a glassworker's shop and just when a basket full of goblets and cut-glass ware was in front of him he swung his staff round and broke them. Whereupon he [their owner] arose and seized him, saying to him, "I know that I cannot obtain redress from you, but come and I will show you how much valuable stuff you have destroyed." Thus He showed them how many generations they had destroyed.

—Genesis Rabbah 19:6a

It is tempting to read the parable of the broken glassware as a way of cutting the first sin down to size. The dimensions of the event, the comparison of human disobedience to the damaging of merchandise, trivializes the act; it suggests, at the least, that nothing of cosmic import happened. Even a king, so familiar a figure in parables that involve God, is lacking; there is little that communicates the high drama of temptation, sin, guilt, punishment, and mortality. Our *midrash* might even be deliberately undercutting the myth of the Original Sin and all that it implied.

I am not sure this reading is really correct—and not only because this glassware is expensive and delicate. Pottery and glassware often suggest the basic human condition, and God, beginning with biblical accounts, is a potter who shapes a human creature of clay. Finally, it is the glassmaker's response, after all, that carries the message—not the circumstances surrounding the event.

Yet even if we grant all this and do not make any claim about the ostensible triviality of the situation, we are puzzled—in part, because the parable is vague at crucial points. Why does the villager break the glassware? Is his being a villager, perhaps unaccustomed to expensive goods or even resentful of them, relevant? Is he less accustomed, being a villager, to carefully walking city streets on which merchandise is spread? Or does his identity as a villager only explain his poverty (so that the owner of the glassware knows that he can't expect recompense)? And how did it all happen? Was the glass smashed maliciously, an act of hostile vandalism—or did the villager simply catch his staff accidentally (or negligently) in the wares spread out in front of the shop?

What does all this mean in terms of the sin of Adam and Eve, the *nimshal*? What happens if we transmute all these questions and rephrase them in terms of the first human sin, or sin in general? It is notoriously difficult to work out the relationships of *mashal* and *nimshal*, to cross "the shifting sands that lie between the narrative and the *nimshal* . . ." (D. Stern). True, the "fit between a good parable's application and its setting is never perfect; when it is, the *mashal* is either predictable or tendentious. . . ." Do our questions simply demonstrate how "the Rabbis plant inequalities and inconsistencies between the *mashal*'s narrative and its *nimshal*"? Or is this *mashal* apt, revealing perspectives on that sin? "The *mashal* deliberately gives the impression of naming its meaning insufficiently. It uses ambiguity intentionally . . . by shrewdly incorporating suggestive openings for the questioning of meaning. . . ."

These questions are sharpened if we take the reading "blind man" (*ivroni*) in place of "villager" (*iyroni*) seriously. This reading is found in only one manuscript, but it flourishes in later re-tellings of our *midrash*; so that even if it is not the original reading (as I suspect), it is a legitimate subject for our reflections. If we read "blind man," the parable suggests a positive answer to the—no longer rhetorical—question: "Were they then blind?" We understand whence the "staff," and we also know why there can be no recompense. Indeed, we can hardly have an angry glassmaker—anguished, yes, but not angry. But what of our *nimshal*? Are we to understand that Adam and Eve are no more guilty than the blind pedestrian, unaware of the glassware that lies at his feet? That they are innocents with whom God cannot even be angry, although they have violated His command? One point is made, however, by portraying humanity as blind (as my son Avraham pointed out to me)—we never really know how often our actions affect eternity, much as the blind man never fully sees the glassware he has smashed.

Perhaps, more prosaically, one must also know when not to expect the coherent parallel, when to admit that the lack of fit indicates that no fit is to be sought, so that the point of the parable lies simply in its second half—in the glassmaker's response (though I must caution that the entire *mashal* up to that point seems too large a chunk of narrative to disregard). Indeed, it is the response alone that the *midrash* itself rephrases in terms of Adam and Eve ("thus He showed them . . .") and that connects to the "opening of their eyes" in the biblical verse. Yet our reducing the "relevant" section of the parable to the glass-maker's (and hence God's) response to the damage does not fully solve our problem either. For even this response, as the *midrash* describes it, is far from the mark of the biblical narrative. Either something is awry, or something else is being said.

∾

The glassmaker mourns his loss, but even when he seizes the villager (who seems strangely rooted to the scene of the mishap), he is not vindictive. He knows it will do him no good to be vindictive—he cannot obtain compensation. Punishment, per se, does not seem an available option, perhaps because the law does not provide punishment for damage done. Out of either exas-peration or sadness, the glassmaker simply confronts the villager with his own deed and shows him the beauty and worth he has destroyed. Why? So that he should not repeat the act, that he be more careful in the future? Or in order to share his own sorrow with its cause? One thing is clear: the glassmaker wishes to teach the villager, not to punish him; and compensation is out of the question.

This, then, according to the *midrash*, is how God treats Adam and Eve after their sin. He shows them ("their eyes were opened") the results of their deed, the "destroyed generations." The mean-ing of this phrase is not immediately clear. Does it refer to a different, more pure humankind that would have been born had sin not intervened? Does it simply refer to all those who would have been born had Adam and Eve retained eternal life? Or does it refer to present-day humanity, whose life comes to an end because of sin? (The identical phrase is used again, when it is said that the Evil Urge "destroyed the generation of Enosh and of Noah's Flood and of the Tower of Babel"—that seems to refer to their moral and spiritual degeneration. But elsewhere it is also said that God eliminated 974 generations that were originally destined to come into being.) In any case, God's pedagogy is the same: He teaches humankind to mourn and to feel guilt. We cannot "repay" Him: What He lost is too great, our abilities are too limited.

But in the biblical story, God does, in fact, punish as well. He does not, cannot, "obtain redress" from humanity, it is true; and, in that sense, the parable is accurately represented in its application. But God does punish, thus behaving differently from either the glassmaker in the parable or the God of the midrashic application. Are we then to explain that the *nimshal* is not meant as an exact "fit" to the *mashal*? That, in distinction to the glassmaker, God also punishes?

Perhaps, this explanation is correct, although the *nimshal* is true to the *mashal* to the end—for, despite the seeming harshness of God's judgment of the sinners, he does not inflict the punishment with which he threatened them: they do not die when they eat of the fruit, nor when they are arraigned before Him. What God does do, the *midrash* insists, is create a sense of the loss and devastation engendered through sin. He bestows (or inflicts) a knowledge different from the type that Adam and Eve thought they would acquire. Adam and Eve will die as a result of their sin and they will toil while they live, but they also know what destiny they have brought upon their descendents.

After all is said and done, the "fit" is suggestively imperfect. This is possibly an aspect of the general gap between *mashal* and *nimshal*, or it may reflect the more specific gap between man (in the parable) and God (in the application). It is not merely that God punishes, while the glassmaker does not; it is rather that the *mashal* creates a tale of property damage to represent a story of disobedience. Nevertheless, the point remains that the *midrash*, in characteristic rabbinic fashion, wants to describe God as

teacher, not as judge, or at least to teach that punishment is
secondary to instruction.

ᐳᐸ

The physical eyes of Adam and Eve are not literally opened, of
course, nor are they granted physical sight ("were they then
blind?"). They are given an inner vision and know more about
themselves and what they did. This understanding persists in the
next *midrash* as well.

Actually, the *midrash* expands on the biblical image before it.
Consciousness of nakedness ("they knew that they were naked"),
the shame that led to the immediate sewing of clothing, is a
matter of social awareness, of personal self-consciousness, not of
physical fact. So, too, the quality of personal alienation, the distance from each other, which is necessary for a sense of nakedness, an alienation that, paradoxically, resulted from the act they
did together. The biblical usage is ironic; the serpent had convinced Eve that when she and Adam would eat of the Tree, "your
eyes will be opened and you will be as God, knowing good and
evil." They do eat and their eyes are indeed opened and they do
know, now, that they are naked—in a sense, the knowledge of
good and evil, as the serpent had promised.

Thus, the *midrash* does not really add anything new to the
Bible's "opening" of their eyes. It is the object of the vision, that
which they "see," that is new. Humanity, according to the *midrash*,
does not sense nakedness alone; it now knows of sorrow and
guilt. Perhaps "nakedness" is already, in this *midrash*, a symbolic
term; perhaps it already suggests an awareness before which there
is no defense or cover. But then, we wonder, of what use are the
clothes Adam and Eve sew? Can the nakedness of guilt be
hidden? Apparently not, for when Adam and Eve hear the voice
of God walking in the Garden, they hide their newly clothed

bodies in the trees, seeking deeper and deeper cover. Physical clothes are, it is clear, no solution at all. They apologize to God that they are naked (fig leaves are not very adequate . . .), but we suspect that it is not their nakedness they hide, but themselves, their very being. They hide in the forest much as Jonah hides in the bowels of the boat.

GUILT

"And they knew that they were naked . . ." Even of the one precept which they had possessed, they had stripped themselves.

—*Genesis Rabbah* 19:6b

The metaphor of nakedness, nakedness as symbol: does the *midrash* believe that Adam and Eve were physically naked at all—or is it all allegory?

The *midrash* is faithful to its own literary insight, though. If the nakedness of humankind refers to our guilt, then it cannot be described as our natural state or even as something we enter passively. Rather, we will have made ourselves naked. Scripture describes the pair as opening their eyes to the fact that they were naked—and had been so from the start—but the *midrash* says that they "stripped themselves," in the active mode.

Guilt, moreover, is *total* in this situation. There is a single command—not to eat of the fruit—and one either abides by it or violates it, thus determining one's moral status completely, radically. That is not how matters will remain: later there will be

613 commands, so that one can have a much more varied and complex conscience, a welter of virtues and guilts. Yet the basic intention of the *midrash* is upon our souls, here and now, and it means to be suggestive in our post-Sinai situation. Apparently, then, we can recognize the image of total, radical nakedness despite the knowledge that we are a moral and spiritual mosaic.

The subtle midrashic hint of the 613 commands to come ("they stripped themselves of *even* the one command they had") has a different point, though. The very term *mitzvah* ("command") calls up the people Israel and reverberates with that which is still in the historical future yet already exists in the memories of both God and reader. Thus, the *midrash* not only functions to describe the state of the guilty sinner, assimilated as he or she is to the paradigmatic sinners in Eden. It also, and contrarily, wishes to establish the gap between those sinners and its contemporary audience, to remind God, as it were, (and to reassure the reader) that Adam and Eve could not remain faithful to the single easy requirement He laid upon them. But His people Israel, it implies, will accept 613 commands—and remain faithful. Adam and Eve now become a midrashic foil for Jewish existence; elsewhere, as we shall see, Adam and Eve prefigure Jewish experience, almost participate in it.

We have backed into the halakhic mode, the normative mind, as it were. The experience of Adam and Eve—temptation, sin, guilt—is all packaged into the quantified objectification: "one *mitzvah*." The Bible itself did, of course, speak of God "commanding" Adam and Eve not to eat of the fruit; and there is no doubt that this characterization of humankind's primary—though not exclusive—experience of God, is symptomatic and formative of the entire biblical tradition and the Judaic understanding of our experience of God. But is this living, encountered command the same thing as "one *mitzvah*"?

It is tempting to say no, to object that the transition from verb to noun is decisive, that reifying the overwhelming experience to a quantifying numeral turns epic poetry into prose. Perhaps, though, we do not hear the full timbre of *mitzvah*, even a solitary one, with all its repercussions.

THE FIG TREE: CONSPIRACIES AND CLOTHING

> *"And they sewed the leaves of the fig [te'enah] together." R. Simeon b. Yohai said; "That is the leaf which brought the occasion [to'anah]—for death— into the world." R. Isaac said: Thou hast acted sinfully: then take thread and sew!*
>
> —*Genesis Rabbah* 19:6c

R. Simeon ben Yohai thinks, along with others, that Adam and Eve not only made their clothes out of fig leaves, but that the fig was the fruit with which they sinned. The very fact that the fig's leaves were used to cover their nakedness was not an accident or without implications; nor were its leaves appropriate merely because of their adequately large size. R. Simeon justifies this identification by a wordplay on the Hebrew name of the fig. A more charming tale is spun by R. Jose:

> What was the tree whereof Adam and Eve ate?
> R. Jose said: They were figs. . . .
> This may be compared to a royal prince who

sinned with a slave girl, and the king, on learning
of it, expelled him from the court. He went from
door to door of the slave girls, but they would not
receive him; but she who had sinned with him
opened her door and took him in.

So when Adam ate of that tree . . . he appealed to all the trees but they would not receive
him. What did they say . . .? "Let him not take a
leaf from me." But because he had eaten of its
fruit, the fig tree opened its doors and received
him. (*Genesis Rabbah* 15:7)

(Once again one asks, How far is one to take the *mashal*? Did the
fruit that was eaten participate in the sin?) However, a straightforward reading of the biblical text itself leads away from the fig
tree. By introducing the fig tree only after the sin, the Bible suggests that, on the contrary, its leaves did not come from the Tree
of Knowledge.

R. Simeon presents a naturalistic reading: the tree was a
familiar botanic phenomenon that remains part of our natural
experience. Others, who suggest that the fruit was wheat, or the
grape, or wine, or the citron (*etrog*), take essentially the same
tack. This discussion, however, focuses on the Tree of Knowledge
alone. No one undertakes a naturalistic identification of the Tree
of Life. Indeed, the only discussion we have about that tree
suggests a near-mythic entity. The Tree of Life "was a tree which
spread over all life." R. Judah b. Ila'i said, "The Tree of Life
covered a five hundred years' journey, and all the primeval waters
branched out in streams under it." Clearly, there is no tree in
existence that bestows eternal life, and so a mythic tree is the only
possibility. The Tree of Knowledge, though, need no longer grant
knowledge or have any special properties; since Adam and Eve
ate of it, benefits have already been bestowed on all humankind.

Even so, the identification of its fruit with wheat by some rabbis does lean on the association of wheat with knowledge.

The Bible itself does not identify the tree or its fruit. Despite the obvious gap that this left in its narrative, the Bible may have preferred to cultivate a surrealistic, dreamlike atmosphere, or not to distract the reader from its central focus by giving too many concrete details. The tree is called the Tree of the Knowledge of Good and Evil, nothing more. Biblical gaps are legion, and the usual midrashic strategy is to fill them in. In our case, as we have seen, some rabbis rose to the challenge and attempted to identify the seductive fruit. But others took the biblical silence as deliberate—and pedagogic. It was not an invitation to interpret, they felt, but instruction in the virtue of concealment.

> R. Azariah and R. Judah b. R. Simon, in the name of R. Joshua b. Levi, said . . . The Holy One, blessed be He, did not and will not reveal to man what that tree was.
>
> For see what is written: "And if a woman approach unto any beast and lie with it, you shall kill the woman and the beast" (Leviticus 20:16). Now if man has sinned, how did the animal sin? But it is killed lest when it stands in the marketplace, people should say, "Through this animal so-and-so was stoned."
>
> Then if the Holy One, blessed be He, was anxious to safeguard the honor of Adam's descendents,

> how much more is He anxious to safeguard
> Adam's own honor! (*Genesis Rabbah* 15:7)

Therefore, the Tree of Knowledge is not identified as the fig tree, so that the fig should not perpetually remind us of Adam and Eve's sin. There is a virtue in protecting the reputation of even the guilty. Naturally, that sensitivity should have led the biblical author to utter silence, for the very story of the Garden of Eden, as told and as repeatedly read and studied, has made the sin of Adam and Eve household knowledge. Moreover, the inference from the moral of normative behavior, killing the beast, to the later moral of literary behavior—masking the tree's identity—is far from smooth. And the analogy of fig to beast also seems odd; it would appear that the fig is here protected, not Adam and Eve.

Be this as it may, R. Joshua b. Levi's point is clear. There is an ethical standard that takes priority over curiosity and the hunger for information. The ethical expresses itself here in the imperative of protecting the reputation of even the guilty from constant befouling. Obviously, others—such as R. Simeon b. Yohai in our case—insist on filling in the gaps. Another interesting case in point is the debate between R. Akiba and his associates about the identity of the Israelite caught collecting wood on the Sabbath (Numbers 15:32). R. Akiba identified him as Zelophehad, father of the daughters who appealed their case to Moses (Numbers 27:1–5); but he was assailed: "Akiba, you will pay a price: if you are right, God nonetheless concealed his identity, and how do you reveal it; and if you are wrong, you have simply defamed the innocent!" It is likely that this topic is part of the broader rabbinic discussion about the priority of truth-telling over other values—in contexts that usually involve personal hurt and human pain.

By and large, though, the information supplied to fill in biblical gaps carries some ethical or religious freight; it is not simply factual. This is true—though not exclusively—even when no personal hurt is involved. The rabbinic project, despite its obvious intellectualist bent, has a strongly pedagogic thrust, and this finds frequent expression in midrashic teachings.

ఞ

The name of the fig tree—*te'anah*—reflects the sin in which it participated. The Bible proclaims the identity of the forbidden fruit to those who have an ear for allusion. And, rather than merely identifying the fruit, the biblical name characterizes it in terms of the disaster it wrought. The fruit carries its disgrace as a linguistic mark of Cain. The Hebrew name, moreover, may refer to either the result of the sin or to its cause, as we shall see. Perhaps, R. Simeon b. Yohai even reads not *aleh*, meaning "leaves" (of the fig), but *ilah*, meaning "cause," (as in Daniel 6:5–6), for the nonvocalized Hebrew text lends itself to either reading. This, then, would render the verse as "they sewed the cause of death together. . . ." Strange to say, the four letters that form the Hebrew name of the fig signify three phenomena, any (or all!) of which could be the referent of R. Simeon's comment:

> (A) *Sexual passion, or lust, as in Jeremiah 2:24 ("a wild ass . . . whose passion* [to'anatah] *none can restrain")*—Midrashic identification of the sin with sexuality—illicit or licit—is later than R. Simeon; generally, in fact, the point is made that there neither was nor is any connection between sexuality and sin. But some Jews were identifying the two with each other in Second Commonwealth times, long before the time of R. Simeon b. Yohai. Perhaps he hinted here that there was something to the idea? Using the leaves of the fig tree to cover nakedness and shame disclosed through sexuality would close the circle.
>
> (B) *Sorrow, as in Isaiah 29:2 ("there shall be sorrow*

[ta'aniyah] *and sighing"*)—In this, R. Simeon would seem to
be closer to the rabbinic consensus and to the biblical text
itself. True, a variety of sorrows can compete for recognition,
depending largely on how one sees the relationship between
this sin and death: the introduction of death; humankind's
inability to escape the mortality inherent in its creation from
dust; the sorrows of physical toil, childbearing, and rearing;
and the frustrations and struggles in the marital relationship—the curses laid upon Adam and Eve.

(C) *Pretext or excuse, as in Judges 14:4 ("He was seeking a
pretext* [to'enah] *against the Philistines"*)—The sin of Adam
and Eve was therefore only an excuse for God's imposition
of mortality, a pretext for that which He had designed for
His creatures from the beginning of creation, but for which
they can themselves be held (somewhat deceptively) responsible. This is a midrashic complaint, from a time later than
R. Simeon's, to be sure.

∾

"Come and see the works of God/Who is awesome
through pretexts" (Psalms 66:5; so would go the
midrashic translation).

R. Joshua b. Korha said . . . when God created the world, He made the angel of death on the
first day . . . and Adam was made on the sixth
day. So Adam was falsely accused of bringing
death into the world when God said, "On the day
you eat of it, you shall surely die."

A parable of someone who wishes to divorce his
wife . . . When he goes home, he takes the bill

of divorce with him . . . and looks for an excuse to give it to her. So he says, "Prepare something for me to drink." She pours for him; but as soon as he takes the cup from her, he says, "Here is your divorce." She says, "Where have I sinned?" He says, "Leave my house. You poured me a luke-warm cup." She says, "And did you know before-hand that it was going to be lukewarm, so that you wrote out the bill of divorce and brought it with you?"

So, too, Adam said to God, "Merciful One, 2,000 years before You created the world, the Torah was already Your companion . . . and it was already written, '. . . when a man dies in a tent . . .' (Numbers 19:14). Now, if You hadn't already prepared death for all creatures, could You write that? Rather, You simply want a pretext to blame me."

So, too, with Moses' sin . . . and Joseph's sale to Egypt by his brothers. (*Tanhuma, Vayeshev* 4)

Despite the midrashic insistence on God's having entrapped humankind, neither the biblical "prooftexts" nor the domestic parable necessarily prove the plot. (Once again, then, the parable does not provide an exact fit for its application, and the daring, ironic, midrashic assertion goes beyond its ostensible source.) Our narrator explicitly tells us that the bill of divorce was, in fact, prepared before the husband went home. Indeed, the human husband had no way of knowing that his wife's soup would be lukewarm—as the wife notes. Yet God does have this advan-tage—in midrashic thought, at least—He does know what His creatures will do, and He can therefore prepare an adequate response. Indeed, a frequent midrashic assertion is that God prepares the medicine before He sends the illness. Even God's antecedent creation of death, then, could be justified as a response to the human sin He foresaw.

That is precisely the idea that R. Joshua b. Korha refuses to entertain, insisting as he does that God devised death before the first human sin had taken place, apparently as part of His definition of creaturely existence. It is clear that R. Joshua spoke from a profound conviction about the deep structure of reality, and a willingness to berate God for imposing on naive humanity its burden of guilt for a reality it did not create. R. Joshua does not offer a re-reading of Genesis; he does not suggest an alternative interpretation of the text. Rather, he insists that God did not tell the truth in Genesis. True, God has not entirely concealed that truth: He made it available to the attentive reader of Psalms and the creation story, and to the possessor of midrashic traditions in general. But Psalms itself, midrashically understood—a courageous midrashic understanding, which itself is in the best tradition of Job and Abraham—virtually accuses God of dissimulation and unfairness.

Moreover, the introduction of death is not the only instance of divine misrepresentation. Joseph's brothers were not really responsible for his sale to Egypt; and Moses' death in the desert was not the product of his sin, either. Certainly, these are cases in which the biblical texts themselves suggest divine manipulation. In Joseph's case, God had notified Abraham of the impending slavery of his descendents and had sent Joseph the dreams that set the brother's plot into motion; Joseph himself, moreover, consoled his brothers (in somewhat ambiguous circumstances) that he was sent to Egypt by divine providence, not by their wickedness alone. And a close reading of the different tellings of Moses' death reveals their variety, not all of which focus on his sin. Yet that is not the perspective of this *midrash*. R. Joshua does not claim to present a closer and more accurate reading of the biblical text. Rather, it insists that the biblical text does not tell the full story, that it misleads.

The *midrash* leaves a number of problems unaddressed. Why should God so mislead? Why does He burden humanity and individuals with a guilt that is not truly theirs? Were Joseph's brothers completely innocent?

∾

"Take thread and sew" is also a legitimate response to sin. R. Isaac proposes that Adam and Eve quite literally made clothes for themselves, and he probably understands their newly-discovered nakedness with a similar literalness—in contrast to the more symbolic and metaphoric meanings to which we have become accustomed.

Yet, by defining "sewing" as the response to sin, R. Isaac shifts the biblical focus. There is more to sewing clothes than providing cover for nakedness. Indeed, it is the sewing, the very activity of *making*, which is the significant fact, not the clothes that are made or the embarassing problem they are designed to solve.

The actual relationship of the "sewing" to sin is not very clear. Is some symbolic statement being made, nevertheless? Are we to understand that the sinner atones by mending the fabric he tore, restoring the wholeness he destroyed, much as the mystics chose to be cobblers so as to join the "upper" with the "lower"? This is hardly hinted at in the *midrash*, nor do the initially separate fig leaves, joined to provide clothing, serve as an apt symbol.

It seems no less likely that sewing represents labor, as if to say that sinning humankind accepted a life of toil, anticipating, as it were, God's explicit curse ("By the sweat of your brow . . ."). Adam and Eve knew that they had sinned, and began to inflict their punishment upon themselves. R. Isaac does have a voice speak to them, saying ". . . take thread and sew," but the speaker is not identified. Is it God? Their conscious? In the Bible, their act is spontaneous, their own choice.

Another possibility suggests itself, something between our first reading of sewing as restoration and our second one of sewing as punishment. The *midrash* is actually quite terse and matter-of-fact; it might be rendered, "You messed up, now take your thread and sew." The point would then be that sewing is neither symbol nor punishment. It is simple, constructive activity. The proper response to failure, even to sin, lies in the return to worldly activity. Adam and Eve are neither to brood nor agonize; they respond in concrete terms to the new situation in which they find themselves. When you discover you are naked, the first thing to do is provide yourself with cover, not theorize about your predicament.

CLOTHING
AND CULTURE

"And they made themselves girdles [hagoroth].*" R. Abba b. Kahana said: Not* hagorah (a girdle) *but* hagoroth *[plural] is written: now* hagoroth *implies shirt [or embroidered girdles], robes, and linen cloaks; and just as these are made for man, so for woman are made girdles, hats, and hairnets.*

—*Genesis Rabbah* 19:6d

The nakedness discovered by Adam and Eve was, superficially at least, physical. The midrashic clothing of R. Abba b. Kahana, too, is made of real stuff. Nevertheless, he takes the primal garments as answering much more than the basic human desire for protection against the elements. Rather, they signify a response to other needs.

For R. Abba b. Kahana, the biblical verse already differentiates between clothing for men and clothing for women—thus, clothes have an initial significance beyond their function of protecting against the elements. Clothing, especially for men, comes in a variety of forms—shirts, robes, cloaks—that do not serve a clear, pragmatic function. The women's clothing mentioned is, in large measure, decorative. (Can we detect a bias?) And fig leaves are only the beginning: neither the men's cloaks nor the women's hairnets are made from fig leaves.

All this, it would seem, is implicit in the initial sartorial thrust. Seemingly functional, clothing, in reality, serves other needs and responds to other claims. Indeed, clothes were not first devised to meet physical needs, such as protecting against the cold and so on. The Bible, after all, does not speak of these needs, which would have been as pressing before the sin as after it; nor do the pair yet know that they will be cast out of Eden into a "cold world." Or, to present a more nuanced view, even clothes that provide protection will serve other functions. The Bible merely tells of the perception of "nakedness"—and that, as we have seen, can refer to a wide range of human realities. By describing clothing as he does, R. Abba indicates that clothes are a cultural phenomenon, not a physiological necessity.

∞

It cannot be accidental, either, that many of the items named by R. Abba have Greek and Latin names—that is, that they are identified with the pagan culture of the time. It is difficult not to hear the critical timbre of R. Abba's comment. These clothes are not merely superfluous; they are also alien, the product of a culture with which Jews have a long account. The comment is double-edged, then. Romans are identified as the inheritors of the sinful characteristics of humankind, in this as in many other areas—Romans and their Jewish imitators.

Indeed, it is hard not to hear an echo of Isaiah's list of the sinful clothing of the daughters of Zion (verses that contain, incidentally, some of the very items mentioned by R. Abba in his list of men's clothing!): ". . . their anklets and the fillets and the crescents; the pendants and the bracelets and the veils; the headtiers and the armlets and the sashes and the corselets and the amulets; the rings and the nose-jewels; the aprons and the matelets and the cloaks and the girdles; and the gauze robes [*gilyonim*] and the fine linen [*s'dinim*] and the turbans and the mantles" (Isaiah 3:18–22). Yet, given the fact that this tendency is already found in that first human couple, it also seems that we are dealing with a basic human propensity, one to which we are all susceptible and almost fated. One may hear negative echos and pick up critical ricochets, but there is no overt criticism.

So this jaundiced view of fashionable indulgence is not the only rabbinic word. Consider this statement: ". . . in . . . rabbinic culture, ornamentation, attractive dress, and cosmetics are considered entirely appropriate to the woman . . . not only are Eve's ornaments a positive gift of God to the man but they are invested with the most positive symbolism that the culture can muster" (D. Boyarin). A husband is also obliged to provide his wife with attractive clothes for festivals. It is almost as if the Rabbis approve of the sexual function of ornamentation, primarily for woman, but disparage its function as social emblem. Foppishness is not Jewish; it derives from pagan influences, or, at best, from a weak, sinning humanity.

EARTH, HISTORY, HOLINESS

R. Abba b. Kahana said: Not mehallek *but* mith-hallek, *as written here, which means that it [repeatedly] leaped and ascended. The real home of the* Shechinah *was in the nether sphere; when Adam sinned, it departed to the first* rakia' *[firmament]; when Cain sinned, it ascended to the second* rakia'; *when the generation of Enosh sinned, it ascended to the third; when the generation of the Flood sinned, to the fourth; with the generation of the separation [of tongues], to the fifth; with the Sodomites, to the sixth, with the Egyptians in the days of Abraham, to the seventh. But as against these, there arose seven righteous men: Abraham, Isaac, Jacob, Levi, Kohath, Amram, and Moses, and they brought it down again to earth. Abraham [brought it down] from the seventh to the sixth, Isaac from the sixth to the fifth, Jacob from the fifth to the fourth, Levi from the fourth to the third, Kohath from the third to the second, Amram from the second to the first, while Moses brought it right down below. R. Isaac said: It is written, The*

> righteous shall inherit the land and dwell [*wayy-*
> *ishkenu*] therein for ever *(Psalms 37:29): then what*
> *are the wicked to do—are they to range in the air?*
> *What it means is that the wicked did not permit the*
> Shechinah *to dwell on earth.*
>
> —*Genesis Rabbah* 19:7b

Whatever theological problems it may cause, R. Abba b. Kahana takes Genesis 3:7 to mean that God Himself moves in the Garden; Adam and Eve hear Him there, not the sounds He may make from a distance. Nor is R. Abba even interested in the philosophical embarrassment caused if God Himself walks. True, he will attribute this activity to the *Shechina*, God's "presence," but the term was used more to signify an aspect of God's reality on earth, rather than in order to distance the actual Godhead from earthy activities. Indeed, R. Abba distinctly wishes to assert God's presence on earth, among men and women.

Now God is not merely walking in the Garden, as is His wont. He is leaving; He is going into self-imposed exile even before His creatures are driven out. Here, in a sense, the *midrash* prefigures later kabbalistic motifs of God's withdrawal, but this midrashic withdrawal is not cosmogonic but ethical. God is taking the first in a series of leaps that will remove Him further and further from human society. To put it more accurately, God departs because He cannot remain. So it is humankind that, by its actions, determines whether God makes His home here or not. In R. Abba's daring imagery, God leaps from one heaven to the next in order to distance Himself even further from an ever more corrupt humanity.

God, then, goes into exile. He is not *returning* home by leaping back to heaven; He is *leaving* home. God, it seems, created the world not as a habitat for His creatures alone, but for Himself as well: "the real home of the *Shechina* is below." Indeed, it almost seems as if His desire for a earthly home was God's major motive for creation itself. This, of course, is just another way of saying that the world was created for righteousness' sake; but the image chosen—where does God make His home?—is strong and concrete. It is also unusual: To the degree that the Bible ascribes an earthly habitat to the Lord, it is the Holy of Holies in the Temple. R. Abba claims, in a sense, that the world is also intended to function as a Holy of Holies, not by virtue of ritual sanctity, but by virtue of human righteousness. So, if "God is in His heaven," it is a telling sign that "all is" not "well below." The authentic realm of the spirit is on earth, where men and women can do the good, not in heaven.

∞

Human history, indeed, is a tale signifying God's withdrawal (or ejection) from the earth and His return. This is the pulse, the systole and diastole. True, R. Abba presents matters rather schematically. Since there are seven heavens, we will find seven sinners and seven righteous men. God takes seven leaps away and then returns in seven stages. His movement is not dialectical; He goes straight up and straight down. Even Noah does not provide a respite for God; Noah's society was primarily one of sinners (which is why it was destroyed), and that determined matters. At the same time, God displayed the forbearance for which He is famous—He did not leap back to the seventh heaven immediately with the first sin, but hovered in the vicinity and only gradually withdrew. There is an ethical message in God's demonstrative patience, to be sure; but the materials available for the homilist also dictated the structure of his narrative. In reality, though, the image of God's leaving and returning, the depen-

dence of His absence and presence on human deeds is the heart
of the matter, and that may be dialectical indeed (as absence and
presence coexist in the confusion of human affairs) or even
radical.

In R. Abba's history, the focus is on the people Israel. It is
Abraham who first succeeds in bringing God closer to humanity—he is the first righteous person. God returns fully when He
gives Israel the Torah through Moses; Moses, then, brought not
only the Torah down to earth but God Himself. And, if God has
remained since then, it is only because the Torah is present—
both physically and existentially. He would not risk it alone. Yet
even R. Abba undoubtedly understands that the struggle is
unending. The roster that begins with Abraham and ends with
Moses perhaps characterizes the continuing vocation of Israel,
not its successful culmination. It is hard to imagine a triumphal
rabbi.

R. Isaac makes it clear indeed that matters are not settled
or simple. He cites Psalms 37:29—certainly post-Sinaitic—as
teaching that the wicked "did not permit the *Shechina* to dwell on
earth." Psalms is perennially true. God is always leaving and
arriving in response to human deeds.

That the wicked do not "permit" God to be present is a strong
statement indeed, suggesting that God was simply run out of the
world, or, in other terms, that God finds it impossible to share the
world with the devil. Indeed, another *midrash* has it that God
cannot stay where an arrogant person lives: "There is not enough
room here for both of us." This is not primarily a reasoned,
deliberate judgment on His part. He simply cannot tolerate
arrogance. There is no room for compromise here.

As is frequently the case, God does not impose Himself; he
acquiesces to human behavior. This is essential for the existence
of human freedom. God could destroy the world of humanity in
order to make ethical room for Himself, but the world He wishes

to live in is precisely . . . the human world. So rather than end matters by imposing the solution His power allows, He withdraws and enables another day to dawn, facilitating the time He can return. Ironically, then, R. Isaac asserts that the wicked cannot be denied their place in the world, ". . . what are the wicked to do—range in the air?" But that is precisely what God will suffer, so to speak, since He finds no room on earth.

∿

By reading "the *Shechina* leaps from the garden," rather than "walks in the garden," R. Abba apparently detaches this clause from its context. The sentence in its entirety states that having heard the sound of God walking in the Garden, Adam and Eve hid from Him. Now, however, the casual connection of the two clauses disappears; humans are not threatened by God when He ignores them. Students have long realized that *midrash* takes the liberty of treating clauses and even words and letters as autonomous units—what Heinemann called "atomization"—seeing each such unit as containing a full measure of content. Thus, the meaning given by the "natural" flow of the sentence is not the only meaning entertained by *midrash*. There may be many ways by which this form of reading is legitimated; let us at least recall that the Bible, as written in the scroll, is not punctuated or graphically divided into sentences at all. It is simply raw text.

This is probably what happens in our case, as well; the ostensible sentence is rephrased as two distinct clauses, although the second one then floats rather freely. God leaves the Garden, and Adam and Eve hide. But one should not rush to this conclusion. Perhaps R. Abba also suggests a different connection between the clauses? This reading would then say that Adam and Eve seek shelter precisely because, and when, they realize that God is leaving, that He is abandoning them. God, then, is more fearsome in His absence than in His presence, no matter how threatening that presence may be. The simple analogy is to children, who would rather face a punishing parent than confront the reality of a parent who is abandoning them:

> "'It is a fearful thing to fall into the hands of the living God'; but to fall out of the hands of the living God is a horror beyond our expression, beyond our imagination" (Donne, *Sermon* 26).

By leaving the Garden, moreover, God ironically announces that Adam and Eve have succeeded. They have, in fact, become "as God"; they can manage their own affairs and therefore need Him no longer. This little demonstration makes its point. Adam and Eve are immediately reduced to their proper stature. They run away.

DEFERRED
PUNISHMENT

R. Berekiah said: For wayyishme'u ("and they heard"), read wayyishmei'u ("and they caused to hear"): they heard the voice of the trees saying, "Lo, the deceiver who deceived his Creator!" R. Hanina b. Papa said: For wayyishme'u read wayyashmei'u: they heard the voice of the ministering angels saying, "The Lord God is certainly going to those in the garden" [to punish them]. R. Levi and R. Isaac differed in their interpretation. R. Levi said: [The ministering angels were exclaiming], "He of the garden is dead [and gone]." R. Isaac said: [They exclaimed]: "Does he still go about!"

Said the Holy One, blessed be He, to them: ["He will die] Le-ruah Ha-yom," that is, le-rawah ha-yom (after the day's respite): "behold, I will give him the day's respite. For thus spoke I to him: 'For in the day that thou eatest thereof thou shalt surely die' (Genesis 2:17). Now ye do not know whether that means one day of Mine or one day of yours. But behold! I will grant him one day of Mine, which is a *thousand years, and he will live nine hundred and thirty years, and leave seventy for his children,"* as it is written, The days of our years are threescore years and ten *(Psalms 90:10).*

—*Genesis Rabbah* 19:8

It would seem that the sound of God is the only sound to be heard in the Garden, and that God's is the only other presence there. Nor are any words reported. Adam and Eve run to hide as do children who, left alone and given their instructions, break the jar while pilfering the cookies, and now hear the first sounds of their parents coming home. For the *midrash*, though, many words were spoken (and heard); virtually every descriptive term in the biblical text is transmuted—atomized?—into part of a conversation. So God's is not the only voice; many speakers are on the stage. The Garden erupts into sound, almost all of it accusing humankind. Could Adam and Eve have perceived it all as refractions of God's anger, as "the sound of God walking in the Garden"?

❧

For R. Berekiah, it is the trees that spoke, the trees whose fruit Adam and Eve were permitted, even commanded, to eat, and the fig from which they took leaves for covering—perhaps even the Tree of Knowledge. Does R. Berekiah have any biblical warrant for making the trees speak, though? There are some possibilities. The sound, after all, comes *le-ru'ah ha-yom*, which can be literally rendered "by the wind of the day"—the wind swirling in the trees, creating sounds. This is suggestive, but more naturalistic than *midrash* usually is. More significantly, the biblical text says that Adam and Eve hid from God in the trees—an odd tactic, if the trees accused them. Perhaps, then, we must read (and the Hebrew permits this!): "they hid from God *who was* in the trees," which not only "solves" the immediate problem but also explains how R. Berekiah could foist an accusing role on the trees to begin with. *Midrash*, then, not only atomizes—it also creates new, larger units of meaning.

It has also been pointed out (by *Maharzu*) that it was the very same R. Berekiah who told how the trees refused to give Adam and Eve their leaves for clothing, saying then the very same thing they say here: "Lo, the deceivers who deceived their creator," until the fig was willing to help (Genesis Rabbah 15, end). Perhaps, then, our *midrash* simply repeats the earlier story? In that case, the voice of the trees continues verse 7 (which describes the making of clothes from the fig); therefore, verse 8—which loses its beginning and end—would simply state "The man and his wife hid from the Lord God."

The other rabbis cited in this passage all have the angels speaking, a feat of textual legerdemain that requires even greater midrashic dexterity. (Actually, the meaning of the midrashic text itself is none too clear, for it can be translated in a number of ways; the Soncino version, which I have used, captures most of the possibilities, though.) For R. Hanina, the "sound" is the voice of the angels, who tell of God's "walking," that is, going to the Garden to punish the sinners. For R. Levi and R. Isaac, "the Lord God" is exclamatory, as the angels address God, informing Him, as it were, that his favorite, Adam of the Garden, is dead, or asking why he is still alive and walking about after what he did. *Mthalekh* is detached from God, assigned to Adam and Eve, and split into two words, one of which is "dead" (*mt*).

Yet it will not do to neglect the narrative just because midrashic technique is so fascinating. For now the narrative has turned dramatic—the Garden is full of characters, all of whom were present at the creation. In this midrashic reading, God must now justify His not bearing down on Adam and Eve, for not punishing them as He had threatened. That is the brunt of the angelic charge, and that is why Adam and Eve hide in the forest. They imagine that the angels have won, and that God will fulfill His threat.

∾

Angels have a traditionally jaundiced view of humans in the midrashic tradition. They opposed their original creation and later opposed Moses' receiving the Torah for the people Israel. In both of these cases, God overcame their opposition: in the former instance, by out-maneuvering them, and in the latter, by requiring Moses to answer their arguments. By and large, angelic opposition focuses on human failings and weaknesses, as compared (implicitly, at least) with angelic perfection. It has been claimed (by Alexander Altmann and others) that these materials reflect ancient tensions between Jews and gnostics; but, be that as it may, we now read them detached from their historical origins. As such, they reflect a basic undercurrent of skepticism about humanity's legitimacy and claim to existence, as measured by our failings and the evil we do.

Three interpretations relate to the angelic response to human sin. Each requires a slightly different reading of the biblical text, but what they hold in common is central for us. All point—either by direct statement or rhetorical question—to the anticipated death of humankind. Given the original angelic prediction that humans were a bad bet, certain to disappoint their maker, it is difficult not to hear in these comments a triumphal undertone. Indeed, when God finally brings the flood, the *midrash* has the angels explicitly reminding God how events have confirmed their original prognosis.

In our case, the matter is even more ironic. The angelic certainty of humanity's end is based on God's original threat to bring death upon Adam and Eve if they eat of the Tree. So God is not merely being reminded of his misplaced faith in humanity; He is expected to declare His project a failure and personally bring it to a close. He should keep His promise, and Adam and Eve should die—that is what the angels demanded.

We know, of course, that Adam and Eve don't die—at least, not then in the Garden, immediately. God's failure to exact the punishment He imposed, His indifference to His own threat— the matter isn't even raised in God's argument with His creatures—has always puzzled readers. One convenient solution is to assume that God did not threaten to bring death to Adam and Eve, then and there; rather, he threatened them with mortality itself—and He does impose that punishment. There certainly are *midrashim* that choose this option. However, it has always struck me that they fly in the face of the text itself, for when God says "On the day that you eat, you shall surely die," He means exactly that. And this is only the most striking objection.

The midrashic solution before us appears in a number of slightly different versions. One explicitly admits that God simply relented, or, to put it more accurately, that He placed the most lenient interpretation possible—a midrashic interpretation—on His original threat:

> "Remember, O Lord, Your compassion and Your mercies/for they have been of old" (Psalms 25:6) . . . the mercies with which You dealt with Adam. For You had said to him, "On the day that you eat of it, you shall surely die." Had You not given him one day of Yours, which is a

thousand years, how could he have begot descendents?

—Midrash Tehillim 25, 8

Without God's generosity, it would not only have been Adam and
Eve who would have died. Humanity as a whole could never
have come into existence. But the crucial teaching here is that
God simply relented, that He did not exact the punishment He
could have imposed. A pattern has been established that will
accompany the dealings of God with man (and, especially, Israel)
throughout history. Yet God's leniency, in this case at least, is not
simply bestowed. It emerges from His midrashic manipulation of
His own threat. For God's day, as opposed to both human time
(and angelic time, as well—a good reminder to the angels of their
own status!) is a thousand years, derived midrashically from
Psalms 90:4: "For a thousand years in Your sight/are but as
yesterday. . . ." These lines from Psalms 90:4 are therefore the
midrashic key to Genesis 2:16.

Midrash is not merely a rabbinic activity; God applies these
very same techniques to His own words. God not only studies
Talmud, as the Talmud has it; He also reads the Bible midrashically. God is both author and reader; both have become divine
activities. Nor is this reading an automatic, "objective" process.
God's "reading" is informed by His mercy; it is a reading that is
guided by its goal. At the same time, even God's "mercies" are
impotent to alter Adam's fate, were there no text to read and no
possibility of a lenient interpretation. It is only because His threat
specified that death was to come *bayom* ("on the day"), which He
can interpret in terms of His *yom* of Psalms 90, that the day of
punishment becomes an occasion for leniency—as *ruah ha-yom*,
the "breeze of the day," will be vocalized *revah hayom*, "the day's
leniency, or flexibility"). In this triple repetition of *yom*, all echoes
can be heard, all meanings can be exploited.

In our *midrash*, God claims that He was wise enough to phrase His original threat ambiguously, an ambiguity present only to the midrashic consciousness, to be sure. The angels did not notice the original ambiguity at all. Their time, as we have seen, is identical with human time, and they were clearly ignorant of the midrashic possibilities of Psalms 90:4. It is difficult not to pick up God's puckish delight in their discomfort. Yet God's leniency is not denied: "I will grant him one day of Mine." God, after all, could have chosen either meaning of the ambiguous *yom*.

It has been fairly possible to treat Adam and Eve, all along, as historical characters, or at least as historical as the products of any miraculous process. This is not said of the believer alone; I am referring to the claim made by the body of writing we are considering, literary logic. There is an element of Everyman and Everywoman in first man and woman, but that does not deny their historical reality; it simply asserts their basic humanity. Mutuality, sin, anger, recrimination, cooperation, punishment— this is the stuff of life itself. Naturally, the more archetypical Adam and Eve seem, the more their concrete reality is suspect. All in all, though, both Bible and *midrash* walk a thin line.

This line is crossed, I think, when the *midrash* accounts for the lifespan of men and women. Each of us gets seventy years, the residue of the term unused by Adam. He had been granted one of God's days, that is, one thousand years; but he lived only 930, thus leaving "seventy for his children." But bestowing seventy years on each human being demonstrates their non-historical character; Adam's years, considered realistically, could be given only once. (This difficulty is inherent, perhaps, in the very notion of transferring "one's" time to somebody else.) Adam, then, is not merely archetype. He is, for this *midrash* (and others, too), the mythic source of human life.

∾

The divine manipulation of Adam's years is fascinating in its own right. God does not choose (let us assume that He could have provided appropriate biblical verses for the necessary midrashic process!) to give Adam seventy years and have each person simply copy the Adamic pattern—as would have happened in a truly archetypical situation. People, on the contrary, live those years that Adam did not. In a sense, each of us completes Adam's life. Put differently, Adam's life has an infinity of conclusions—another aspect of his fundamentally mythic character.

God, moreover, gives Adam one thousand years, only to then take some back, which He gives to Adam's decendents. And, in distinction to other well-known tales, Adam does not volunteer these seventy years; they are simply appropriated for his children. Yet these irreverent observations aside, a more basic pattern is disclosed: the process of giving life to children is sacrificial. It is only by losing some of his years, after all, that Adam can guarantee his descendent's life. At this point, we cross from the mythic back to the archetypical, or to the symbolic, sphere of discourse.

There is another charming ambiguity in the description of this entire sequence. It would seem as if Adam himself repeats the process begun by God; he leaves seventy years for his children, just as God "granted him one day of Mine." This is obviously not the case, though. God's day is not "His" in the sense that He is deprived by granting it; it is merely defined by Him. Nevertheless, it does seem that God is the model for Adam in the larger sense, for both Adam and his creator provide the years necessary for life to continue. God outwits the angels, and Adam gives of his own substance. If God is "trickster," Adam, too, must pay a price.

HUMANKIND
AND THE
PEOPLE ISRAEL

R. Abbahu said, in the name of R. Jose b. R. Hanina: It is written, But they are like a man *(Adam),* they have transgressed the covenant *(Hosea 6:7).* "They are like a man *(Adam)"* *means like Adam: just as I led Adam into the garden of Eden and commanded him, and he transgressed My commandment, whereupon I punished him by dismissal and expulsion, and bewailed him, with* ekah *(how)! (I led him into the garden of Eden, as it is written,* And the Lord God took the man, and put him into the garden of Eden *(Genesis 2:15); and I commanded him:* And the Lord God commanded the man *(Genesis 2:17); and he transgressed My commandment:* Has thou eaten of the tree, thereof I commanded thee that thou shouldest not eat *(Genesis 3:11)? and I punished him by dismissal:* Therefore the Lord God sent him forth from the garden of Eden (Genesis 23); and I punished him by expulsion: So he drove out the man (Genesis 24); *I bewailed him with* ekah *(how)! And said unto him:* ayyekah (ekah *is*

written): so also did I bring his descendants into Eretz
Israel *and command them, and they transgressed My*
commandment, and I punished them by sending them
away and expelling them, and I bewailed them with
ekah! *I brought them into* Eretz Israel, *as it is written,*
And I brought you into a land of fruitful fields
(*Jeremiah 2:7*); *I commanded them:* And thou shalt
command the children of Israel (*Exodus 27:20*),
also, Command the children of Israel (*Leviticus
24:2*); *they transgressed My command:* Yea, all Israel
have transgressed Thy law (*Daniel 9:11*); *I punished*
them by sending them away: Send them away out of
My sight, and let them go forth (*Jeremiah 15:1*); *by*
expulsion: I will drive them out of My house (*Hosea*
9:15); *and I bewailed them with* ekah: Ekah (how)
doth the city sit solitary (*Lamentations 1:1*).

—*Genesis Rabbah* 19:9b

Adam and Eve have clearly served as symbols for all humanity
thus far. We all recapitulate their experience in one way or
another; their hopes, temptation, and sin are the stuff of life.
True, we have not touched upon those midrashic materials
dealing with the punishments leveled on them, their banishment
from Eden, and their ultimate death, but it is obvious that these,
too, are the basic experiences of all men and women, the
existential realities we all share. We are all driven from Eden.
Adam and Eve are universal figures whose experiences are
encoded in the lives of all mankind.

Without necessarily denying this personal focus—as *midrash*
can accept the polysemous nature of the biblical text—R. Jose b.
R. Hanina places the foundational experience of Eden in a dif-

ferent context, that of the national experience of the people Israel. Entry into Eden, divine commandment, temptation and sin, banishment: all of these forebode the career of the Jewish people. This is not necessarily to say that only the people Israel are the "true" descendents of Adam and Eve—an assumption that may be debated elsewhere—but simply to read their story as prefiguring the Jewish experience and to read the Jewish experience as already being present in the foundational human experience, perhaps even to give a universal dimension thereby to the particular Jewish instance. This reading also puts a slightly different spin on the biblical narratives of both Eden and Israel. The Land of Israel, in almost Eliadean terms, becomes a recapitulation of Eden, and life in the Land is a renewal of Edenic existence. The Land loses some of its naturalistic, geographic character and takes on more mythic colors. The assimilation of the Land to Eden also requires a more specific shift: the people are commanded *after* they enter the Land, in this telling, much as Adam and Eve are commanded after they are placed in the Garden; in the Bible, though, the commands precede the entry to the Land and are given in the desert. All this firms up the significance of the Land for the Jewish saga.

Yet the story of Adam and Eve also shifts, ever-so-subtly. Broadly put, the centrality of the Garden now parallels the centrality of the Land of Israel; it is not merely background to a story of temptation and sin. Moreover, the midrashic story now stresses even the very moment of entry into the Garden as being parallel to the entry of the people into the Land, a formative and crucial component of the ongoing discourse with God.

We are reminded that Adam was not both created *in* Eden, much as the people Israel was not created in its land. Adam was formed in some unspecified place outside the Garden and was placed there later by God, while Eve was taken from his body after he was already in the Garden (Genesis 2:15–22). One may well ponder the significance of this differential creation: Adam outside the Garden (thus the parallel to Israel's entry into the Land), Eve in it. On the purely biblical level, it seems that *neither* Adam nor Eve could be created *of* Eden: Eden is the native land of no human being. And since Adam was to be created out of the land, that meant he had to be made outside Eden; otherwise, its earth would serve as his body. But Eve's body was taken out of Adam, not directly out of the earth, so the geographic provenance of her creation becomes perhaps much less significant. Yet, given the sensitivity of the question and the suggestivity of biblical texts, other solutions are more to the point: other meanings may certainly surface. Nevertheless, the "outside" world brackets Eden/the Land Israel. Just as Adam/Eve/Israel were created outside their Eden, so may they be compelled to return to their place of origin.

Commandment and sin are the basic experiences within Eden and the Land. This is patent for the national component of our parallel. It is also a likely way of reading the Eden story, as we have already had occasion to point out. By assimilating Eden to the Land, it becomes conditional, something that Adam and Eve have to earn continually, the prize that they must constantly win, the home that is always at risk and from which they may be torn, the symbol of divine approval they must merit.

And, finally, Exile. Despite the significance of the curses laid upon humanity by God, it is clear—even without midrashic illumination—that the banishment of Adam and Eve from their home in the Garden is the truly powerful close of the narrative. It is the only thing that actually happens, the only concrete event, the only real image with which the reader is left. Everything else is talk. The centrality of banishment is strengthened all the more when it coincides with the national experience of the people. And *that* experience now shares in the universal, existential narrative.

Banishment becomes the universal mode of punishment, the content of all human fears, both personal and collective.

Yet the midrashic elaboration of the biblical text, its introduction of the national theme, also opens up the Edenic narrative and provides it with an alternative conclusion. For the biblical message to the people Israel is that they will be redeemed and returned to their Land, that Exile is only temporary. What of the Exile of Adam and Eve? Is that, too, only temporary; is humankind, too, destined, to return to Eden? Is that why we are always trying?

∾

Indeed, Exile is not God's final word in the midrashic narrative. There is one more touch, and there Eden is assimilated to the Land of Israel. In the biblical text, as it is normally vocalized, God asks Adam: *Ayeka?*, "Where are you?" Now, other midrashic texts will suggest numerous ways of explaining God's apparent "ignorance" of man's whereabouts; in truth, God's questions are always a topic of great suggestiveness. One typical gambit is to read the question symbolically, that is: "Where *are* you?" "Where"—what point have you reached? How did you get to this juncture? *Who* are you, now?

Our *midrash*, though, changes the vocalization. *Ayeka* becomes *Eykha*, the term with which the Book of Lamentations begins: "How sits solitary the city/that was full of people!" (Note that R. Yose does not cite the alternative use of the term by Isaiah [1:21]: "How is the faithful city become a harlot!") God mourns the exile of Adam and Eve from the Garden, much as He mourns the exile of His people from their Land. God does not punish triumphally, vengefully, or spitefully—or even angrily. He cries as He gets a glimpse of an empty Eden.

∞

Hosea 6:7, with which our *midrash* begins, compares Israel with Adam. The primary topic, then, compares people, not places. God does not mourn the Land, or the city, or the Garden—He mourns the people He created who have betrayed Him, as the verse in Hosea concludes.

By portraying Himself as perennially betrayed, from the very beginning of His dealings with humanity until His disappointing experience with His people, God is asking for our sympathy. This, too, is our response to His tears.

Something is also being said about the condition of both Israel and Adam. Israel, we hear, repeats the basic human pattern, almost preternaturally, almost fated to self-destruction. Yet why is Israel presented with the same challenge failed by Adam and Eve? Isn't it because there is new hope in the divine breast? Perhaps even hope that Israel can redeem the earlier failure?

And Adam and Eve: there is always something remote about the attitude of the Jewish tradition to these two. They are always held at arm's length, as it were. Although human, they are "other." They are not our parents alone, but the parents of all humanity. So they belong to the family, but not on intimate terms. R. Jose b. R. Hanina tells a different story, though. Adam and Eve are our forebears not only on the personal level, but also on the national one. Their experience prefigures ours fully, and so they are drawn into the family circle. Perhaps, too, Hosea says, we should have learned from them?

HUSBANDS
AND PANDORAS

*"And he said: I heard thy voice . . . And He said:
Who told thee . . ." (Genesis 3:10–11)? R. Levi
said: Imagine a woman borrowing vinegar, who went
in to the wife of a snake charmer and asked her, "How
does your husband treat you?" "He treats me with every
kindness," she replied, "save that he does not permit
me to approach this cask which is full of serpents and
scorpions." "It contains all his finery," said the other;
"he wishes to marry another woman and give it to
her." What did she do? She inserted her hand into it,
and they began biting her. When her husband came,
he heard her crying out [with pain]. "Have you
touched that cask?" he demanded. Similarly, "Hast
thou eaten of the tree, whereof I commanded thee?"*

—*Genesis Rabbah* 19:10

The woman borrowing vinegar is obviously interested in more
than that—her borrowing vinegar is a ploy to get into the home,
where she will pursue her other interests. Metaphorically, she *is*

103

after vinegar, of course—of a human sort. And so she poses her question. One imagines that the average wife would find the query intrusive and inappropriate—adequate reason for showing its author to the door. This wife prefers to answer, however. From her answer, we learn that she has already decided that her husband has unjustifiably denied her something, that denying her the contents of the cask is the very opposite of kindness. Carrying these sentiments around within herself, she is primed to complain, indeed welcomes the opportunity. The question "How does your husband treat you?" merely releases what is waiting to escape.

The wife's worst fears, not unexpectedly, are now confirmed. The vinegar-borrower not only asks innocent questions and gathers information; she is also able to dispense it (undoubtedly on the basis of information gathered elsewhere). The husband, she reveals, not only lies to his wife and denies her the contents of the cask; the cask and its contents are simply an expression of his basic unfaithfulness to her. The wife then plunges her hand into the cask, probably in order to confirm her worst fears and prepare for the coming stage in her relationship with her husband and possibly even to spitefully enjoy what he had prepared for her rival. But the husband, it transpires, had been telling the truth all along.

Does the vinegar-borrowing woman know this from the outset? Not likely, as no special prescience is attributed to her. She is, rather, worldly-wise, shrewdly understanding the human reality she confronts. She assumes that the husband who is so caring is, in fact, considerate to the end and tells his wife the truth: the cask does hold scorpions. But learning that the wife suspects her husband, she promptly attacks at the weakest point. A proverbial meddler, she is willing to disrupt the home (which, in any case, shows some fissures); she is even willing to expose the wife to actual physical danger.

The husband is beyond reproach. He isn't at home to protect his wife from such rumor-mongers, but then, why should he be? And why should he suspect his wife's faith in him? He had treated her with loving concern. Not only had he permitted her access to all the other casks, he had warned her of the contents of the dangerous one, forbidding her to approach it—paternalistic as that might be. He was not testing her loyalty to obedience—that cask really was full of serpents, as he had promised. Why have such a cask in your home? Well, you are a snake charmer. . . .

The "fit" of the parable is, once again, moot. Perhaps one should simply say that the only true point of contact between *mashal* and *nimshal* is that which the *midrash* renders explicit, namely, the nature of the question asked by the snake charmer/God ("Have you touched?"/"Have you eaten?"); all else is merely introductory narrative. Yet the other alternative beckons. Indeed, our parable exists in two other versions, both of which differ at crucial points in their application to the biblical narrative; clearly, something was at stake. So we legitimately ask: What results do we get if we attempt a point-by-point parallel of *mashal* and *nimshal*?

The snake charmer equals God. Certainly, the basic image of God as a spouse to humanity, an image undoubtedly based on the dual grounds of covenant and love, is significant. Thus, He is not only a parent to his childlike creatures. He, too, has left instructions while he is absent: the command not to eat of the Tree of Knowledge. The snake charmer does not appear to be testing his wife; on the contrary—he must keep snakes about, and he wants to protect her while he is away. That is to say: he is the source of danger, but he also tries to control its potential for harm. One must then say that the Tree of Knowledge is banned, not in order to test or selfishly to deprive humankind of something that would benefit them, but because it is truly, objectively harmful. We are not told, however, why such a Tree exists to begin with, if it is not a device by which humankind will be tested. The snake charmer needs his snakes about, after all; why does the divine creator "need" a Tree of Knowledge in His Garden? Here, once again, we encounter the gap between the earthly parable and its application to the divine sphere and its doings.

All this presumes that we translate h-v-r as "snake charmer." These same letters, though, can be read as "scholar," or "one who is religiously punctilious." That would create a completely different basis for comparison and would even suggest readings of the parable itself. A pious husband has no need of a caskful of snakes, so one must conclude that he keeps them in order, eventually, to test his wife. But why should a husband test his wife? Does the vinegar-borrowing woman's question uncover—knowingly or not—an old wound? All this, of course, would find its obvious parallel in the instructions given in Eden by God, Who is now simply testing His creatures, no more. It is difficult to dismiss this reading out-of-hand. Other *midrashim* distinctly utilize a parable of a *haver* ("scholar") and his wife in our context. It is also questionable whether a snake charmer actually works with both snakes and scorpions.

The vinegar-borrowing woman represents the serpent. The serpent, much as did the meddlesome woman, begins his foray with a question, an ostensibly ingenuous and even concerned question but one that is obviously designed to draw Eve and Adam to a sorry end. Should we suggest that he, too, is not really informed about the nature of the Tree of Knowledge but simply exploits Eve's revealing conversation? He, too, will play on jealousy and insecurity: God's instructions are not meant for your good, but for His; He even intends, as we saw in other *midrashim*, to continue creating other and more precious creatures.

Who is the snake charmer's wife? The simplest approach would be to identify her with Eve, of course, taking account of the obvious sexual correlation. This identification would also tap into a more subtle motif. We have already noted Eve's fear that Adam would find a new companion for himself, and it is this identical fear upon which the vinegar-borrowing woman plays in our parable. *Mashal* and *nimshal* would then converge in one narrative.

Against all this, however, stands the fact that the midrashic parable is appended to God's question of *Adam* (in the biblical text): ". . . Have you eaten of the tree . . . ?" The logic of our text, as it stands, is clear: the snake charmer's wife represents Adam and Eve *both*—indeed, primarily Adam. The serpent's blandishments, indeed, appeal to all humankind; perhaps, the "other woman" of the parable even represents the insecurity and fear common to all humankind, which other *midrashim* have explored. And so the *mashal*, by presenting a wife as the character who disobeys instructions, may suggest a false *nimshal*; and so we must consciously disentangle the strands of rabbinic *mashal* and biblical *nimshal*. The character of the snake charmer occasions a similar tangle. On the level of *nimshal,* he translates as representing God, who, in some undisclosed way, is responsible for the true serpent in the biblical narrative, the one who, in fact, wounds Eve and Adam. It is indeed tempting to argue that the antithetical use of snakes in the biblical narrative and the rabbinic parable—making the serpent both tempter and avenger—is itself deliberate and suggestive. On the whole, though, rabbinic parables don't work that way.

∾

Two other versions of the parable exist. The differences between all the versions suggest that their authors did, in fact, expect some sort of "fit" between *mashal* and *nimshal*, but that they disagreed as to what it should be.

Here is one alternate version of the parable:

> . . . to what may Adam be likened? To one who had a wife at home. What did that man do? He went and bought a jar and put into it figs and nuts, a definite number of them. Then he caught a scorpion and put it at the mouth of the jar. The jar he sealed with a tight-fitting lid and put it in a corner. "My dear," he said to her, "everything I have in this house is in your hands, except this jar, which you may not touch at all."
>
> What did that woman do? As soon as her husband left for the marketplace, she arose and opened the jar, and stuck her hand into it—and the scorpion stung her. She started back and fell on her couch. When her husband returned home from the marketplace, he exclaimed: "What is this?" "I put my hand on the jar," she replied, "and a scorpion stung me; and now I am dying." "Did I not tell you so in the beginning," he demanded, "everything I have in the house is in thy hands, except this jar, which you may not touch at all?" Forthwith, he grew angry with her and sent her away.
>
> This is what Adam was like when the Holy One, blessed be He, said to him, "Of every tree . . ." When he ate of it, he was banished. (*Abot de-Rabbi Nathan* (A), Chapter 1 [trans. J. Goldin, pp. 12–13])

In this parable, too, the wife represents both Adam and Eve and the husband represents God. So it is the behavior of the husband (who equals God) that is significant—not his identity. Why does he forbid the jar to his wife? And, more to the point, why does he protect it with a scorpion?

Does "a definite number of figs and nuts" signify (as the phrase often does) expensive fruit, which the husband wishes to deny his wife? But this husband allows his wife the enjoyment of "everything I have in this house" (save the nuts and figs!), and even stresses his largesse to her. It is unlikely that these fruits are so precious, then. And using the scorpion as the husband does is certainly harsh. He is not, after all, a snake charmer who has scorpions around as a matter of course; this scorpion is placed deliberately at the mouth of the jar to punish anyone—undoubtedly, the wife—who reaches in, as well as to disclose the culprit. The husband is not merely protecting what is precious to him. "He went and bought a jar and put into it figs and nuts"; he is scheming. The sealed jar is a test of obedience and loyalty, almost of gratitude, a test that carries its own punishments. The wife is bitten immediately; but she does not die, for she is also banished from her home.

Applying the parable to the biblical narrative, we realize that the Tree's intrinsic value is hinted at as a parallel to the "figs and nuts, a definite number of them." Yet if "figs and nuts" are precious, so, too, the fruit of the Tree of Knowledge; there is no good reason to deprive the wife/humanity of either. So the Tree and its fruit really serve as the instrument by which Adam and Eve are tested, for God's command to them is primarily a test. It, too, carries its own punishment, just as it marks the culprit: Adam and Eve perceive their nakedness after they eat of the forbidden fruit, and their subsequent fashioning of clothing exposes their sin. And just as the wife's "death"—which is never quite clarified—is not really her true punishment, so, too, with them; after suffering the knowledge that is newly theirs, they, too, are exiled from their original home and, perhaps, lose their original relationship with God, much as the wife's relationship with her husband is severed.

Yet, while a reader may be willing to acknowledge the significance of God testing humanity and setting limits for us, it is difficult to sympathize with the husband in our *mashal*. Is the parable meant, then, to question God's behavior? To suggest that He is tyrannical? Or should we say that these comments are anachronistic, that husbands were allowed such behavior in the ancient world, and that the original reader of this *midrash* would not make our value judgment?

One more perspective ought be introduced. The wife had no intention of actually touching the cask (whatever she may have thought). The husband had correctly gauged her loyalty. He simply hadn't counted on the vinegar-borrowing visitor. So perhaps he should not be blamed too harshly. All discipline courts temptation, of course, but that doesn't make it illegitimate—it only means that it should be used with prudence and wisdom. Can we say the same thing about God and the serpent?

Here is a second, alternative, version:

> . . . To what was Eve to be compared at that hour? To a king who married a wife and gave her authority over the silver and gold and over all his possessions and said: Everything I own is yours except for this jug, which is full of scorpions.
>
> An old woman came calling on her like those who . . . ask for a little vinegar. She said to her: How does the king treat you? She answered: The king treats me wonderfully. . . .

> She reached out and opened the jar: the scor-
> pions bit her and she died.
> The king is Adam. The wife is Eve. The one
> seeking to borrow vinegar is the serpent. (*Abot
> de-Rabbi Nathan* (B) chapter 1 [trans. A. Saldarini,
> pp. 35–6])

In terms of literary history, this telling seems the latest; its
editor even takes the trouble to provide his parable with a key.
Here, again, the husband—now a king—tests his wife. Perhaps
the husband's cruelty is even amplified in this version; by
declaring all his silver and gold hers, he sorely tempts her to
break into the jug—which ostensibly contains something even
more precious. But the application of the parable is greatly
simplified. The king is Adam, not God (elsewhere in *ADRN* (B),
Adam is explicitly called "Eve's king!"). But the most spectacular
difference lies in the identification of the wife as Eve, not
humankind. *Mashal* and *nimshal* are almost collapsed into one
incident, as the fears of the king's wife are identical to those of
Eve, which are described in other *midrashim*.

Pandora's box must, of course, be let out of the jug. The obvious
relationship of our parable to the Greek tale was noted long ago.
The distinctiveness of the midrashic re-working, however, should
also be noted. First, our *midrash* tells its tale as a way of understanding the biblical narrative, specifically, the dynamic of temptation, rather than as a way of explaining how death entered the
world; indeed, no one else but the wife dies. More significant,
perhaps, is the identity of the wife in the *nimshal*. As we have
seen, she is not (except in the oversimplified version of *ADRN*

[B]) Eve, or women in general. She is, rather, Adam and Eve both, humankind as a whole. Both Pandora and the Bible accuse woman of bringing death and/or corruption into the world. So, too, do many *midrashim*. Our *midrash* uses the myth of Pandora but applies it in a strikingly nonmisogynistic way.

SELF-KNOWLEDGE

> *R. Abba said: Not* we-okalti *(and I did eat) but* wa-okel *is written: I did eat and I will eat. R. Simeon b. Lakish said: Adam was not banished from the garden of Eden until he reviled [God] and blasphemed, as it is written,* And he looked that it should bring forth grapes, and it brought forth wild grapes *(Isaiah 5:2).*
>
> —*Genesis Rabbah* 19:2a

In what spirit does Adam assure God that he will continue to eat of the fruit, that is, to sin: in defiance? Or, perhaps, in resignation? This confession comes at a sensitive moment; accused of sin, Adam is expected to express contrition and shame, to resolve to mend his ways—at the worst, to shift the blame. Instead, according to R. Abba, he promises, unflinchingly, that there will be more of the same. Humans will continue to sin. If Adam is not defiant but simply frank, he must be given credit for his insight and honesty. But he does leave God little choice.

Perhaps, though, Adam's "I will eat" ought be placed in its very specific context. He confesses that he will continue to eat, that is, of the forbidden Tree of Knowledge. But that is possible only as long as he remains in the Garden where the Tree is located and where he has access to it. Adam answers God, after all, before he has been exiled from the Garden and, more significantly, before he even knows that he will be exiled. What he may be saying, then, is that as long as he remains in the Garden, he will not be able to resist the fruit of the Tree, even to fulfill God's command. (Certainly, as long as Eve remains with him—and she is the subject of the previous biblical clause.) He is not being wilfull; he is simply admitting his unenviable situation.

A slightly different reading would have Adam speak of the second tree, the Tree of Life. Adam would then be admitting that he ate—of the Tree of Knowledge—and that he will eat . . . of the Tree of Life. Now, God will shortly express that very same apprehension, that Adam will eat of the Tree of Life unless he is exiled from the Garden. Perhaps, then, God's certainty that the pair will eat of the Tree of Life, if they remain in the Garden, is actually a reflex of Adam's own admission.

Whichever reading one prefers, the thrust of Adam's confession and its force are identical. Adam fundamentally gives God permission to exile him from the Garden. Indeed, he sadly invites him to do so, for banishment is the only stratagem that will save him from sinning further: "I will eat." (One almost hears echoes, here, of the talmudic rule that the criminal must accept his punishment in order for it to be imposed legally.) In short, Adam exiles himself.

This expansive and nuanced reading of R. Abba's terse comment is supported by the editorial choice to follow it with R. Simeon's insistence that Adam was not exiled until he blasphemed and cursed God. Banishment was not the automatic punishment for the first sin—it must be justified. R. Simeon says that Adam brought it on himself by continuing to sin. R. Abba would agree that Adam would continue to sin, but his Adam, far from being a defiant figure, basically wishes to be protected from sin and asks God to help him. Exile, then, is God's answer to Adam's request. If Adam permits God to exile him, God permits humanity to leave His Garden.

Adam's admission, his midrashic self-awareness, is probably yet another ironic benefit of his having eaten of the fruit of the Tree of Knowledge of Good and Evil. If the Torah told of humankind's knowledge of nakedness, the *midrash* here tells of its moral self-awareness. But, as frequently happens in both biblical and midrashic narratives of knowledge (compare the end of the Joseph story!), the person who believes he understands does not really see the whole picture—at least, not yet. For humankind continues "to eat" even after its exile from the Garden and that Tree, and after the one command has been transmuted into 613.

∾

Another perspective, although one that is somewhat removed from the literary realities (and religious sensibility?) of the midrashic period: "I will continue to eat"—of the Tree of Knowledge, but in a metaphorical sense. I will continue to inquire, probe, study. This overwhelming appetite, once stimulated, can never be sated. Perhaps, even: I have, in fact, been convinced by the serpent, and I do not repent. Or, Adam asks: Will this always be a sin? Need this always be the message of the serpent? Is this the blasphemy of which R. Simeon speaks?

In this instance, too, a parallel reading is possible: "I will continue to eat"—of the Tree of Life, but, again, metaphorically. Wisdom is described in Proverbs (3:18) as a "Tree of Life for all who hold on to her," in a near-fusing of the two Trees. Thus, humanity, even if driven from the Garden so that it should not eat of the Tree of Life, is nevertheless (and paradoxically) invited to cultivate that Tree.

∾

R. Simeon's claim is unambiguous enough, but it remains vague. When and how did Adam blaspheme? Is R. Simeon describing an event unrecorded in the Bible? There is not even a hint in the proof-text that would provide a basis, even a midrashic basis, for such a claim.

Perhaps Adam's blasphemy is expressed in the very text on which R. Simeon comments: "Adam said, 'The woman you put at my side—she gave me of the tree and I ate.'" Responsibility for the sin is not mine, Adam urges, it is Eve's; and, indeed, it is really Yours, God, for placing her at my side. Not only was she Your idea and gift but, since she came from You, I had no reason to doubt her suggestion (Nachmanides). Adam shifts responsibility from his own shoulders to God, Whom he now accuses of responsibility for his misfortune. This characteristic will become more sinister in Cain, whose "Am I my brother's keeper?" is understood by the midrash to be an accusation of God: "You, after all, watch over us all!"

The blasphemy is compounded by the nature of Adam's accusation. Eve was created after Adam experienced loneliness; her creation is the result of God's concern. It should have occasioned gratitude, but it became a subject for Adam's resentment. Interestingly, Adam is not satisfied with accusing Eve. Nor does he blame the serpent, the much more direct agent of his undoing. (That will be left for Eve to do, for a variety of reasons.) Adam, therefore, is not merely interested in finding a legal excuse or even another being upon whom he can unload his own guilt. Rather, he is interested in accusing God. Thus, even by blaming Eve, by denying his own responsibility, Adam is, in effect, rejecting all of God's world. "Blasphemy" seems to be strong language for these human failings. Perhaps, however, the human refusal to accept responsibility, the perennial desire to blame the "other"—and here, God is the ultimate "other"—is blasphemy indeed.

Furthermore, we can't overlook another aspect of Adam's complaint. There is something childish about it, as he accuses God of betraying him in his dependency. "Blasphemy" is a strong term for such whining. God now sends Adam (and Eve) out into the world, where they will learn that they are responsible for their own fate.

INDEX

Sin (*continued*)
  sewing of clothes and,
    77–78
  sexuality and, 4, 73
  social norms and, 11
Snake. *See* Serpent
Social norms, sin and, 11
Solomon, 15
Sorrow, 73–74
Sotah, 8–9
Stern, D., 58

Ta'aniyah, 74
Talmud, 94
Tanhuma, Vayeshev, 74–75
Te'anah, 73–74
Temple, 85
Temptation, 110–111
Time, 94–95
To'anatah, 73
To'enah, 74
Torah, 86, 92
Tree of Knowledge, 14, 16. *See
  also* Fruit of Knowledge
  Adam and, 50, 113–114,
    115
  danger of, 105–106
  identification of, 69–73
  inquiry and, 115
  as instrument of God's testing,
    109
  power of creation and, 36,
    37

serpent's eating of, 40
touching of, 28–29, 31–32
voices and, 90
wheat and, 70, 71
Tree of Life
  Adam and, 114
  immortality and, 56
  mythic qualities, 70
  wisdom and, 115–116
Trees, voices of, 90–91

Vinegar-borrower's parable,
    103–107
  alternate versions, 106,
    108–111

Wheat, Tree of Knowledge and,
    70, 71
Wife, humankind as, 103–112
Wine, as fruit of knowledge,
    46–47
Wisdom
  anger and, 15–18
  Tree of Life and, 115–116
Woman, creation of, 48–49,
    99–100
Worlds, multiple, 36–37

Yom, 94–95
Yose, R., 101

Zelophehad, 72

About the Author

Professor Gerald J. Blidstein holds a Ph.D. in Talmud from Yeshiva University (where he also received *semikha*) and an M. A. in English and Comparative Literature from Columbia University. He has taught at Stern College for Women, Temple University, McGill University, and, since 1972, at Ben-Gurion University in Beersheba, Israel, where he also served as Dean of the Faculty of Humanities and Social Sciences. Previous books include: *Honor Thy Father and Mother* (1975); *Political Concepts in Maimonidean Halakha* (1983), which won a Jerusalem Prize in 1985; and *Prayer in Maimonidean Halakha* (1994). He is married to the former Batya Max and is the father of six children.